Of
Tithes
And
Testimonies

Of Tithes and Testimonies

Anita Holmes
Johnda Mason Smith

Copyright © 1996 By
HORIZON PUBLISHERS & DISTRIBUTORS, INC.

All rights reserved. Reproduction in whole or any parts thereof in any form or by any media without written permission is prohibited.

First Printing: March 1996

International Standard Book Number:
0-88290-572-4

Horizon Publishers' Catalog and Order Number:
1020

Printed and distributed
in the United States of America by

& Distributors, Incorporated
P.O. Box 490 Bountiful, Utah 84011-0490

Acknowledgements

To the many dear, kind Latter-day Saints who have freely shared the accounts of their trials, tribulations and hard-earned testimonies, we give thanks. Without you, there would be no book! To Duane S. Crowther and Horizon Publishers, who saw merit in our book proposal and have held our hands through the publishing process, we are endlessly grateful. To our families who have supported us from Day One and continue to provide us with ample opportunity to give and receive service in so many forms, we express our love forever and ever.

Table of Contents

Of Tithes and Blessings	9
Three Options	17
Anita Holmes	
Bottled Blessings	23
Johnda Mason	
The Envelope	27
Sandy Patterson	
A Pocket Full of Miracles	33
Cheryl and John Palmers	
Tithe 'n' Save	39
Myke and Bill Mason	
London and Leather Wallets	45
Jane and Claus Gildner	
Life Impacting	51
Scott Shakespeare	
Found Funding	57
Mida and Phil Pedersen	
Single, But Never Alone	63
Paulette Youngberg	
The Phone Rang as They Prayed	67
Jean and Duane Crowther	
Giving Thanks	75
Cheryl and John Palmers	
The Prompting	79
Christine and Curtis Jasper	
No Laughing Matter	85
Jenny Hasty	
We Couldn't Go Just Part Way	91
Golda and Neil Bishop	

"And Prove Me Now Herewith" 97
   Billie and Bruce Sturtevant

Paper Money 101
   Lynnette Boyer

When Less Means More 105
   Adriana Perusia

Always Enough 111
   Mida and Phi Pedersen

A More Sure Formula 117
   Gail and Ralph Lewis

"And I Will Rebuke the Devourer
for Your Sakes" 121
   Glenna and Michael Merket

"Return Unto Me, and I Will
Return Unto You" 127
   Terry and Pat Brame

If, Then 133
   Lorelle Kirby Loosle

Good Things Happen 137
   James Connor Backus

A Burning Testimony 141
   Charity and Scott Shakespeare

A Strong Witness 149
   Sandra and Mick Strong

Attitude, Gratitude and Heavenly Blessings 153

About the Authors 159

Of Tithes and Blessings

Years ago a Relief Society lesson, centering on the law of tithes and offerings, shared the story of an older Irish couple. Missionaries had brought the "good news" to their countryside home in the mid 1930's. The wife was subsequently converted to the gospel, and became a member of The Church of Jesus Christ of Latter-day Saints. Her husband remained a non-member.

In the ensuing years, World War II had a deleterious effect on the lives of most Irishmen. Even if a family did not have a relative or friend fighting the Axis powers on the European front, availability of food, clothing, and other life necessities was marginal. In many humble homes, the question of where the next meal would come from was constant and frightening.

During the war years, the wife faithfully paid her tithing from the earnings of her knitting. Her husband remained silent on the subject of her regular offerings to her church, but his silence itself was a rebuke for what he considered an utter waste of a scarce resource that could be better used to meet daily needs.

At the close of the war, he could no longer refrain from a harsh comment. "Woman, do you have any idea how much better off we would have been had you saved for us the monies you gave to your church?"

She softly but firmly replied, "Man, has it never dawned on you that while neighbors have gone without meals and warm coats, we have never wanted? When others were scrounging for half-decayed vegetables and grains from the field, our potato bin has never been empty. *Not a single meal have we missed* in all the long years of the war."

What a testimony of the unexpected blessings that can come to those who place their trust in the Lord, to those who, out of love for Him, choose to obey His commandments. Commandments, in this instance, which were recorded many times throughout the Bible, but most powerfully so in Malachi chapter three concerning the payment of tithes and offerings:

> Return unto me, and I will return unto you, saith the Lord of hosts. But ye said, Wherein shall we return?
>
> Will a man rob God? Yet ye have robbed me. But ye say, Wherein have we robbed thee? In tithes and offerings.
>
> Ye are cursed with a curse: for ye have robbed me, even this whole nation.
>
> Bring ye all the tithes into the storehouse, that there may be meat in mine house, and prove me now herewith, saith the Lord of hosts, if I will not open you the windows of heaven, and pour you out a blessing, that there shall not be room enough to receive it. (Malachi 3:7-10)

We first find mention of tithes in Genesis chapter fourteen, when Abram paid his tithes to Melchizedek, King of Salem. When Christ re-established His church in the meridian of time, the law of tithing was again re-affirmed. There are references to the practice of tithing in Matthew 23:23, Luke 18:12, and Hebrews Chapter 7. In these latter-days the Lord has proclaimed:

> This shall be the beginning of the tithing of my people.
> And after that, those who have thus been tithed shall pay one-tenth of all their interest (income) annually; and this shall be a standing law unto them forever, for my holy priesthood, saith the Lord. (Doctrine and Covenants 119:3-4)

As in the days of the ancient church, so in the latter-days of the Church of Jesus Christ. President Brigham Young explained, "The law of tithing is an eternal law. The Lord Almighty never had his kingdom on the earth without the law of tithing being in the midst of his people, and he never will. It is an eternal law that God has instituted for the benefit of the human family, for their salvation and exaltation." (*Journal of Discourses* 14:89.)

As a child in Sunday School, President Gordon B. Hinckley learned the following couplet:

> *What is tithing? I will tell you every time.*
> *Ten cents from a dollar, and a penny from a dime.*

While a member of the Council of the Twelve, President Howard W. Hunter defined a tithe as follows: "The law is simply stated as 'one-tenth of all their interest.' Interest means profit, compensation, increase. It is the wage of one employed, the profit from the operation of a business, the increase of one who grows or produces, or the income to a person from any other source." (*Conference Report*, April, 1964, p. 35.)

We may submit our ten cents from a dollar and further offerings as an obligation in fulfillment of a commandment, and consider ourselves better persons for becoming masters over our finances, but we are also promised blessings as we may be in need. The Irish sister did well to see the Lord's hand in the adequate food supply her family received when many others went wanting.

If we pay tithing in the hopes of getting rich, we are doing it for the wrong reason. But if we proffer one-tenth of our income, and other offerings annually, as a consecrated gift—a token return of the portion of the abundance Father has bestowed upon us—we can indeed expect heavenly help in our lives.

What form the help may take is hard to say. Blessings resulting from faithfully donated tithes and offerings are not always in the form of financial or material benefit. We need but understand that Father knows our gravest needs and, as we stretch our hand out to Him—following closely behind faith with works—He will reach out, clasp our hand firmly in His, and help us along the path of mortal life. Has He not told us that . . .

> There is a law, irrevocably decreed in heaven before the foundations of this world, upon which all blessings are predicated,
>
> *And when we obtain any blessing from God, it is by obedience to that law upon which it is predicated."*
>
> (Doctrine and Covenants 130:20-21, italics added)

And, further,

> *I, the Lord, am bound when ye do what I say; but when ye do not what I say, ye have no promise.*
> (Doctrine and Covenants 82:10, italics added)

Is the Lord a liar? Such a thought makes the mind reel! Then, has He not promised that He will "open the windows of heaven according to our need, and not according to our greed"? (President Gordon B. Hinckley, "The Sacred Law of Tithing," *Ensign,* December 1989, p. 4)

Collectively, members of the Church benefited from re-dedication to the law of tithes and offerings under the leadership of President Lorenzo Snow. In 1899, precipitously sunk into debt through the illegal appropriation of church-owned properties by enemies of the Saints, the Church was rapidly losing the ability to meet its growing needs. Inspired to travel to drought-stricken St. George, in southern Utah, the prophet addressed the people there with a powerful sermon. In it, he pronounced the need for the Saints to exercise greater obedience in terms of contributions per the ancient law of tithes and offerings. In return, he promised an end not only to the drought, but to the financial woes of the still young Church of Jesus Christ of Latter-day Saints. In revelation he was told that if the Saints would but live the existing law of tithing, the Church as a whole and the Saints individually would be blessed and their financial problems would be lessened.

Those promises, made by the voice of a prophet, as directed by the Lord, were fulfilled. Tithing continues to be the source of income for the Church to carry forward its many heaven directed activities, even as in ancient days.

Individual promises by the Lord are varied. In Malachi He says,

> *I will rebuke the devourer for your sakes*, and he shall not destroy the fruits of your ground; neither shall your vine cast her fruit before the time in the field . . .
>
> And all nations shall call you blessed: for ye shall be a delightsome land, saith the Lord of hosts. (Malachi 3:11-12, italics added)

The Lord has, in effect, promised us the most precious blessing of health—that he will rebuke death for our sakes. We are taught that when Malachi speaks of the fruits of our ground, this applies to our personal efforts and concerns as well. In modern revelation we also are promised great blessings of wisdom, of knowledge, even hidden treasures of knowledge.

As we approach the dawn of the great millennial day, the Lord has promised, "Behold, now it is called today until the coming of the Son of Man, and verily it is a day of sacrifice, and a day for the tithing of my people; for *he that is tithed shall not be burned at his coming*." (Doctrine & Covenants 64:23, italics added)

Does this mean that if we obey all of the commandments we will forever be protected from bad things happening in our lives? Not for a moment! We are here to learn and grow. "For I have decreed in my heart, saith the Lord, that I will prove you in all things, whether you will abide in my covenant, even unto death, that you may be found worthy." (Doctrine and Covenants 98:14)

We do not necessarily experience overt adversity due to lack of commitment to the commandments, but we do sometimes experience it in spite of obedience to those same directives. The difference is, we will never enjoy blessings from consciously choosing to be disobedient, but we most certainly will from making the effort to be obedient.

While conversing with many of our friends and families in the course of doing research for this book, we came across numerous individuals who have faithfully and willingly paid tithes and offerings for years. But the question of specific blessings as a result of obedience to this commandment left them stumped. One sister remarked, "I cannot tell any particular event which I could attribute directly to my life-long commitment to pay my tithing. But, how can I say that the remarkable marriage I have enjoyed for almost 40 years is not, in ways I do not even realize, a blessing of my obedience?"

Surely in some instances we have experienced blessings for our obedience and faithfulness, but have been too preoccupied by daily life matters to recognize the positive consequences of our compliance! Or the blessing received—not being what we felt we most needed—goes unacknowledged and, ungraciously at best, acquired.

However, precious memories abound of trials of faith successfully met and subsequent blessings enjoyed. Just what blessings have His Saints in current times experienced as a result of paying honest tithes and offerings? This book provides some choice examples.

Three Options

Anita Holmes

"Be happy to put your application on our pile—er, file; we'll be happy, that is, to place your app in our file." And, with that by now rote response, I knew I had been dismissed.

It wasn't that the office manager or personnel director, or whomever I was being directed to in shop after shop, was being rude or even facetious. The simple fact was that every business establishment I entered had already been besieged with requests for employment.

File, or, undoubtedly, pile—its thickness reflected the hopes of dozens of other applicants—for a non-existent position. Totally typical in my two weeks' worth of experience attempting to find a job that balmy September, 1970 in Provo, Utah.

As newlyweds, my husband and I had decided to postpone my education. Instead, I would bring in income to support us while he completed his degree at Brigham Young University.

In theory, this appeared reasonable and prudent. It evidently struck about 10,000 other couples the same way! Immediately after our August wedding we drove our used Volkswagen bug from western Oregon to Utah. We commenced housekeeping in an old home which had been renovated to accommodate five apartments on three levels.

Apartment set-up was actually confined to evenings, while I spent days searching for that elusive job. When I had tracked down all the newspaper leads, a friend and I established a daily system. Simple, and to-date, totally ineffective. But on we went. Doggedly. Choosing a business district, one block at a time, we canvassed communities around Provo. Eileen would apply in store/business number one. I would confidently (ah, hope truly does spring eternal!) enter and make application with store/business number two. Leap frogging our way down street after street, city by city, we eventually made our way to Springville.

Located six miles south of Provo, my first impression of Springville was one of pleasantness. Nestled against the Wasatch Mountains, almost as if in its own little valley, the community seemed old and new all at once. Taking a little side jaunt, we drove leisurely through a residential section. Pioneer homes and newly constructed dwellings rubbed elbows companionably. Returning to the business at hand, we redirected the little red bug to the compact, two block long business district.

As we pulled into the parking lot for the Central Bank, Eileen laid back in the passenger seat. When I reminded her that it was her turn to apply, she announced that it was Friday afternoon, she was tired, and she wished me all the luck in the world. So I drug my body out of the car, and just before entering the bank building, squared my shoulders and adjusted my smile.

No, there are no openings. Sure, we'd be delighted to have you fill out an application form.

As the new account representative pulled out the pile of unsolicited applications, I saw a stack about half an inch thick. Ooooh boy.

That weekend my husband and I spent a lot of time determining our options. School had started, he was working part-time and I was bringing in marginal money by baby-sitting. A quick inventory of our financial and basic living assets tallied three weeks' pre-paid rent, one week's worth of groceries, a full tank of gas and twenty dollars. Our options boiled down to three; pack up and go home; continue looking for a job until the money and food ran out and then go home; or give away our last twenty dollars.

What? Give away our money? Yes! Young, desperate, and trusting.

> . . . Return unto me, and I will return unto you, saith the Lord of hosts. But ye said, Wherein shall we return?
>
> Will a man rob God? Yet ye have robbed me. But ye say, Wherein have we robbed thee? In tithes and offerings.
>
> . . . prove me now herewith, saith the Lord of hosts, if I will not open you the windows of heaven, and pour you out a blessing, that there shall not be room enough to receive it . (Malachi 3: 7, 8, 10)

We decided to take the Lord at His word. Sunday morning we submitted that same twenty dollars as our tithing.

For the remainder of the day our hearts could be found just above our tonsils, but we slept well. I spent the early morning hours cleaning house and deciding where to pick up the job search. About 11 o'clock a.m. the phone rang.

The gentleman on the other end of the line spoke slowly and confusedly. He explained that he really didn't know why he was calling me . . . there were, after all, so many other applications.

I was beginning to wonder if he had the wrong number. He assured me that I was the person he meant to contact. And, while this fellow was still a complete stranger to me, his voice was a curious blend of bewilderment and sincerity.

And, so I met Mr. J. Grant Nielson, owner of a lumber yard and construction company in Springville, Utah. He was in need of a secretary-bookkeeper, and, after mulling over the best way to locate one, had decided to come in to one of the city's banks and browse through their applications. He had dropped in at the local branch of Central Bank, where they were kind enough to allow him access to their file.

As he continued with the who, what and why's of his phone call, he finally reached the how—what he described as the "really puzzling part." He had spread out in front of him over 100 applications. And out of all of them, he had picked up mine, and he "couldn't put the darn thing down."

He was looking at resumes of applicants with twice my experience. Local, permanent citizens, with grown families and nothing to interfere with the job at hand. But, he related, he couldn't seem to get past mine. So, would I be interested in the job?

Would I?! I started that same week, and worked at the Grand Lumber Company of Springville, Utah until the birth of our first child one year later. Mr. Nielson's casual perusal of a pile of unsolicited applications may have been a mystery to him, but there was no doubt in my mind whose hand had placed his over one particular app.

The only truly remarkable thing is not that the Lord kept His promise (why would we ever think otherwise?), but that in later years I have now and then forgotten that, no matter how desperate things get, I can always express my trust in the Lord and receive the subsequent blessings.

BOTTLED BLESSINGS
Johnda Smith

Five ways to identify a shoestring budget:

1. When you can fit your entire financial statement on the back of a postage stamp.
2. When you wear make-up only on the days you go to church.
3. When you make extra-firm oatmeal and mold it into the shape of a turkey for Thanksgiving dinner.
4. When a major shopping spree is going to *one* yard sale.
5. When you find yourself claiming that you *like* to walk all over town carrying a child on each hip.

Like many young married couples, this was our fiscal reality. It wasn't totally unexpected. We knew we'd be poor at first. We had just never translated that knowledge into the mundane rite of daily living.

We had established our kingdom nearly three years earlier and had added two subjects to our population; a prince and a princess. Our second-hand trailer, tucked into a windy hillside of Pendleton, Oregon, was our castle. There we learned to manage our kingdom's resources with industry and ingenuity.

It was evident from the beginning that the resource of money was esoteric and we were not to be among the select group who knew and understood it. Fortunately, happiness was a more universal asset. We generated plenty of that.

In September of 1975, Nick and I called an emergency meeting of the Ministry of Finance. There was a new and unexpected drain on our kingdom's resources. The doctor had indicated that I needed daily medication for the next few months. No amount of creative ingenuity could take care of this crisis. We needed a specific quantity of rare, elusive, and green currency to provide for the medical necessity at hand. It was a little scary.

We talked about it as we pored over our budget trying to find something to eliminate. We could squeeze enough out to purchase one bottle of pills each month. Each bottle contained enough medicine for twenty days. We looked harder for something else we could cut back on. There was nothing. Our eyes rested on the amount at the top of the page; the amount set aside for tithing. Silently we considered it, each thinking, "We could pay it back after this crisis is over."

We raised our heads and gazed into each other's souls. A slow smile spread across our faces and twinkled in our eyes as we simultaneously said, "Naw, that's not ours."

Right then we needed Heavenly Father's help more than ever. It was the worst time to think of cheating Him.

We paid our tithing and bought my bottle of medicine. Each day we prayed for His help and knew we would receive it, for we had kept the law upon which the needed blessing was predicated.

In a couple of weeks only a few pills rattled around in the bottom of the bottle. It made my heart thump harder, and my stomach became an Olympic gymnastic competitor when I realized how long it was to the end of the month, but in prayer I was assured that all would be well with me.

I continued to take my medicine every day, yet the bottle wouldn't empty. There were always a few stragglers left down there.

On pay day I took the last pill in the bottle, paid our tithing, and bought my new bottle. I counted the tablets. There were only enough for twenty days. Yet, again the second month, pills came out of the bottle until pay day.

This went on every month until I no longer needed medication. If the first fell on a weekend and pay day was therefore on the third of the month, it didn't matter. The bottle delivered my daily dosage until we got paid. Additional currency was not required to meet this need.

The Ministry of Finance was still in good health and the Ministry of Health was finally sound. Our little kingdom prospered. Our happiness grew. Our fiscal reality gained an added dimension. We now had certain knowledge that by living the law of tithing we had lifted our small kingdom closer to His, and benefited by doing so.

This form of financial security is not esoteric. It is meant to be understood and used by all.

The Envelope

Sandy Patterson

"Well," Sandy Patterson explains, "The only reason my sweet little mother has not been translated is because just often enough she slips up in some teeny, tiny way that keeps her mortal!" Anyone who has met Fayone Whitehead of the New Harmony, Utah LDS ward, knows just what Sandy is saying. This dear woman taught her five children from their earliest years that paying tithing was not an option.

"Even when our allowance was only a quarter a week, we automatically brought to the bishop our three pennies, and when the allowance increased, so did the amount paid on it. Mother always raised us with such a strong sense of paying our tithing that even in a period of inactivity for me in the Church, I ALWAYS returned that money to the Lord," says Sandy. Even so, the day would come when the decision to return to the Lord was not that easy or automatic. And, in that day, Sandy would again turn to her mother for direction, for Fayone's teachings, both by word and by example, have continued to bless her children in their adult years, and proximity to her offspring has little to do with it.

For Fayone, life turned full circle in 1987 when, upon her husband's retirement, they returned to New Harmony. There, as newlyweds in 1947, they had built their first home, for the incredible sum of $1,100. There, in the eastern morning glow of the huge monolithic rock formations known as Kolob's Fingers, and the westerly evening shadows of the Great Pine Mountain, they welcomed three of their five children. There, Fayone first taught her little ones about the law of tithing.

Their sojourn in southern Utah was interrupted by a thirty-three- year intermission in Henderson, Nevada. Known as the fastest growing town in Nevada, Henderson is just fifteen miles west of Lake Mead and directly south of Las Vegas. It was there that Sandy and her siblings enjoyed the balance of their growing-up years.

In spite of the sterling example of her mother, Sandy's teen years were sometimes darkened by stubborn attitudes. "I would call myself the 'black sheep' of the family, but if I did, my mom would feel the need to say some little thing in rebuttal—just the sort of thing that probably keeps her from being translated—so, let's just say that as a teenager I made some short-sighted spiritual choices."

As adults, the five children established lives in Nevada, Utah and Arizona. Sandy's last two years of high school were spent in a special vocational program from which she graduated with a degree in secretarial sciences. In the middle of her senior year she started working for a law firm which offered her full-time employment after graduation.

During that time she dated a couple of fellows, finally being courted by one young man in particular. However, in 1972 Sandy broke up with this long-time acquaintance. It was traumatic, and a miserable experience for her. Gwen Hughes, her friend, could barely put up with her loneliness, and in desperation introduced her to another acquaintance. He was Bob Patterson, who had also just emerged from a disappointing courting experience and was equally mopey.

It was the proverbial match made in heaven. Six months later, in May of 1973, Sandy and Bob were married. She describes her life companion of twenty-two years as the "dearest, most wonderful man imaginable."

The years with Bob passed swiftly. The couple welcomed two children into their family, sons Bill and Paul. The only cloud on the little family's horizon was Bob's job. His job security was often marred by repeated lay-offs and union strikes at the large industrial firm where he had worked for many years.

By 1980 Sandy was entering her fifth year working as secretary for the Clark County School District. She was also pregnant with their last child, due the twenty-second of October. At least, on paper the baby was due the third week of October. But Sandy knew better than to expect the new little one on the doctor-diagnosed-date. Her other two babies were both long overdue before making their earthly appearance, and she had no reason to think that this one would be any more punctual!

The pregnancy passed smoothly, and an especially hot summer (as always seems the case when one is in the final trimester of pregnancy, regardless of the actual thermometer reading) gave way to the bearable temperatures of September (a mild 95 degrees). It was a month marked by new beginnings for the family: children embarking on new school years, Sandy quitting her job to prepare for the baby's imminent arrival and, unexpectedly, an ending also for Bob's job.

On October first, company employees went on strike. With news of the strike went any hope for medical coverage for the baby; over the course of a strike all employee benefits were lost, along with gainful employment. And it was the now-useless health insurance that the Patterson's had counted on to pay for the baby's birth.

At that point in her life, Sandy kept a very special envelope in her bedroom dresser drawer. Shoved back under clothing items in the early-marriage bureau, it held her cumulative monies for return to the Lord. Without fail, each pay check she received she immediately cashed, separated Father's portion, and then slipped the monies into the number ten, plain-white envelope for safe-keeping. Once a year the envelope and its contents were duly returned to the Lord. Even though this was during a less-active period in Sandy's life, a member of her ward's bishopric lived right across the street, and she had but to deliver her tithes to her neighbor's home for safe delivery to the Church.

Now, the contents of that packet weighed ever-so-more heavily than any scale could ever register. It was the only fiscal resource she could think of to pay for the baby. Sandy needed her stalwart mother's input, and she needed it quickly. She dialed the Henderson number and, to her relief, her mother answered the phone. Fayone listened to Sandy's story of lost jobs and no more medical insurance with a heavy heart. But when Sandy confessed to her mother that she was considering "maybe keeping the tithing money for the hospital bills that are coming up," Sandy says, "my dear, sweet, soft-voiced mother replied in no uncertain terms, 'You grab that envelope and get it over to your neighbor IMMEDIATELY!'." That was really all Sandy needed to hear, the voice of one who had unerringly guided her from her first days on earth. She grabbed the envelope and did as instructed.

Within twenty-four hours of delivery of the envelope, the family received a call from the union. Company management had contacted them, requesting a scant dozen men out of the 500 employees to return to the facility to "shut things down." The task should take only four hours and while they were extending this courtesy to the company, the workers would, of course, be doing so at full pay with all benefits restored for the entire month of October! Would Bob be interested in helping with the shut down?

This was a wondrous turn of events for the worried couple and Bob immediately accepted the offer. However, taking advantage of the reinstated medical coverage would help only if the baby cooperated and was born no more than nine days after the October twenty-second due date. Sandy's most recent birthing experience with Paul was an eleven-day-late-occurrence. Even a birth just one hour after the October thirty-first extension of health benefits would be too late for the couple to be covered.

Daughter Callie was born on the twenty-sixth, just four days over due! Birthing complications doubled the anticipated hospital bill, but the medical coverage took care of every cent. "And I know," says Sandy, "that it was a direct blessing from taking the envelope and its contents over to my neighbor, and being square with the Lord."

For many years now Sandy has been in full activity in the Church, attending the Las Vegas Temple regularly, deeply involved with her children, still partner to this wonderful man who supports her fully in her beliefs and, eternally, daughter to that incredible mother.

A Pocket Full of Miracles
Cheryl and John Palmers

Since John & Cheryl Palmer had met three years earlier in sunny, southern California, their lives had been anything but dull; the adrenaline-drenched adventure of forever trying to meet their week-by-week budgetary needs on a now one-wage-earner-part-time-job was just one of their more exciting challenges!

So Cheryl found herself that late spring afternoon staring incredulously at the outside pocket of her zippered scriptures cover. What she was seeing was impossible . . . right down to the familiar crumpled form of one bill . . . how could it be? The young mother quickly went over events of the last week and came back to the inevitable conclusion that her husband had indeed taken their last seven dollars out of the black pocket for gas money. Or had he? Or was she just losing her mind? Well, she could not resolve the mystery of the money until John returned home from work. As desperately as she needed just that amount to get diapers and food for her two babies, she would need to wait and make sure that John had already used it for transportation. But if he used it, then what was it doing back in the scripture cover, or if he didn't use it, how had he been driving the delivery car for the pizza company for the last week??? The more she thought on it, the more she had a feeling that something wondrous had happened. But it really all hinged on what John had to say. Distractedly she went about the daily duties of attending to her little daughter and infant son, excitedly awaiting John's late-night arrival.

During that torturously long evening, Cheryl had time to reflect on the last few years. In those not-so-long-ago days before she returned to California and met John, Cheryl had been a brand-new BYU graduate. She majored in film, but actually graduated in geography. "That," she explains, "is what happens when you run out of money and just want to finish up on a degree, any degree, as soon as possible!" With her shiny new degree in tow she returned to Turlock where her family now resided. She was the eldest of eight children, all born and raised in the Church. Gospel principles and the good brethren and sisters throughout the west had served as a comforting constant in her otherwise nomadic growing-up years, as the family had followed Cheryl's dad to a series of positions in computer technology with universities in the Mountain States and Pacific Coast regions.

Cheryl immediately found a job working as office manager for an air conditioner company. It was there she first saw her future husband working with a construction crew. She was not back in California long before a young adult branch was formed in neighboring Modesto. There she again ran into John, who was a returned missionary and an active member of the Church. Their courtship was quick and sure.

They were the first fruits of the Y. A. branch, being sealed together in the Oakland Temple in 1989.

John continued working in construction until the building slow-down hit California and he was laid off. He scrambled for a new job, competing with hundreds of other recently displaced workers until at long last being offered part-time work in early '91 delivering pizzas for Pizza Hut. He was bringing home exactly thirty dollars a week. What they really counted on to make ends meet were the tips customers would bestow on John. To this end, he worked his heart out in delivering not just pizzas but fast, friendly service.

Cheryl was now home full time. As a young married couple, their two little ones had wasted no time in arriving—daughter Jessi was followed only eleven months later by their son, Tarl. Cheryl recalls that they were living in a one-bedroom cockroach-infested apartment and that was when the real challenge of paying tithing entered their lives. Even at only three dollars a week, that amount represented a goodly portion of the cost of food for the babies.

The young couple were counting on a sizable income tax return, and they postponed weekly payment of tithes, promising themselves and the Lord instead that it would all be caught up and a full and honest one tenth of their income paid from the return. However, during that time, the gas was siphoned out of their car three times and the registration sticker stolen from their license plates, all at additional expense to the struggling family. Cheryl battled pancreatitis that put her in the hospital, and, ultimately, almost lost her life to the disease. The little family was really looking forward to that tax return and catching up with the Lord, and the blessings it would bring! It finally came and while it was everything they expected—over $1,000—after paying tithing and the outstanding bills, they were once again flat broke. John was still not getting full-time hours from the restaurant, having no luck finding other work, and for some odd reason, the tips that he usually got for pizza delivery inexplicably dried up.

On their meager income, a checking account was not needed. Cheryl developed a habit of carefully taking any cash and stashing it in the outer pouch of her scripture cover.

And the week came when after fixed expenses they had exactly seven dollars left . . . seven ones. One of the dollar bills, Cheryl remembers, was oddly folded over and over and then crumpled "with a weird wrinkle." The little family had two extremely pressing needs for the small sum of remaining monies, and the seven dollars was just enough to meet one or the other need, but not both. Either the money would go to buy diapers for the babies, or would be used to buy gasoline for the car so that John could continue delivering pizzas. They decided that it would be more prudent to use the money for gasoline and hope that the tips would start coming again; with the tip money they would be able to purchase diapers and food to see them through the week. John took the last of their money, including the strangely folded and crumpled dollar bill out of the little pocket, and they symbolically crossed their fingers for tips. He returned that night, the next, and the next after that with nothing.

John left for work late that Thursday afternoon with little hope left. Numb from the reality that their gamble for tip money was not paying off, Cheryl refused to give in to dark thoughts, but instead decided to open the Book of Mormon, looking for strength from the scriptures. As soon as she grasped her scripture holder she felt prompted to look through its now-empty pocket. Talk about desperation! But when she pulled it open, she was dumbfounded to discover the exact same seven dollars John had taken days before for gasoline, even down to the mashed dollar bill.

An eternity later John came in the door. He confirmed that he had indeed taken the money from the holder; how else could he have been driving for the last week? When she showed him the money in the pocket he was amazed, but they wasted no time in thanking the Lord and going to the store for diapers. In that order!

In his book *Faith Precedes the Miracle*, President Spencer W. Kimball explained,

> Being human, we would expel from our lives physical pain and mental anguish and assure ourselves of continual ease and comfort, but if we were to close the doors upon sorrow and distress, we might be excluding our greatest friends and benefactors. Suffering can make saints of people as they learn patience, long-suffering, and self-mastery. (p. 98)

Cheryl Palmer will tell you how true it is.

And what were the fruits of a battle with obedience successfully waged and won? A pocket full of miracles.

TITHE 'N' SAVE
Myke and Bill Mason

Lieutenant Junior Grade Bill Mason frowned at the information in the letter from his wife's new church. He immediately phoned the Bishop of the Alderwood Washington Ward and asked why he was assessed only half the suggested amount for ward budget. The Bishop kindly explained that when the primary wage earner was not a member, the family was not asked for full financial participation in the Church.

"Listen," Bill replied, "My wife and kids are down there every time the doors are open. I have just as much right to pay a full budget as anybody else."

The Bishop graciously agreed and sweetly invited Mr. Mason to pay a full budget donation. His participation would be most welcome. Smiling, the Bishop placed the receiver in its cradle. Myke Mason may have accepted the gospel first, but with an attitude like that Bill wouldn't be far behind.

Bill and Myke were a well-matched pair. Each gave 100 percent to everything they did. Myke had accepted a calling to teach a Primary class with a long list of inactive members. Attendance was now 100 percent. Saturdays often found Myke flying kites in the park with her children—her own and those in her class. Giving 100 percent to the Lord had been her lifestyle long before the missionaries brought the gospel to her. She didn't realize that she was doing anything out of the ordinary.

She felt the same way about tithing. Tithing was part of the plan for her blessing and she joyfully paid a full tithe from her own earnings. It never occurred to her to ask Bill to tithe. When he saw the blessings in their life, he'd do it on his own.

That was the truth! Bill knew a good thing when he saw it! In less than two years, he was baptized. His feelings toward tithing were as clear as his attitude about offerings: it was a privilege and a right.

That attitude served him well, for in 1959 the Masons were transferred to Connecticut where a building fund was added to the list of offering opportunities.

Bill and Myke carefully taught their children to share their attitude toward tithes and offerings. Every week three chubby cherubs lined up at the breakfast bar and received an allowance of ten pennies. Immediately, three round little fingers began pushing pennies across the table: one for the Lord, one for the building fund. They felt very rich with eight whole pennies in their hands. More importantly, they never once thought of those first two pennies as their own money. Those belonged to the Lord.

Living God's laws had to become automatic for this busy family. There was simply no time to waffle! That fall, as soon as Bill was ordained an elder, he was called to serve as first counselor in the Branch Presidency. Myke was serving as Relief Society President, Primary Chorister, Merrie Miss Teacher, and Primary In-service Leader. Commitments of this much time, energy and money required careful planning to keep the family running smoothly and the budget balanced. Myke recalls, "Our donations represented such a high percentage of our income that we were audited by the Internal Revenue Service each of the four years we lived there!"

Above the hub-bub and excitement of all these events was the great opportunity they now had to be sealed as a family for time and all eternity. Accomplishing this goal was their primary focus. It was a long trip to the nearest temple. Maps were pulled out and the calculations began.

Mileage charts showed the most direct route to Salt Lake City was 2,323 miles long. Stopping only for fuel, the shortest possible time needed to travel that distance was forty-two hours and twenty-one minutes. Round-trip for a family of five would cost $150. This figure did not include motel charges. It did include breakfast each morning in a restaurant. Lunch and dinner would have to be created from ingenuity and a cooler. Even so, there was no way to save that much this year.

Bill's salary as an instructor at the Coast Guard Academy wouldn't stretch that far, even with the extra income Myke brought in by teaching cake decorating classes. They already lived as frugally as possible, shopping only at the submarine base in Groton. The prices at the commissary and exchange on the base were very low. In fact, they were even lower than the sale prices at any other retail outlet. There simply was no way to cut expenses. If only there was more time. But there wasn't.

In addition to his teaching duties, Bill coached the Coast Guard Rifle/Pistol Team. Summers were spent on tour. That left only the Christmas break for the Masons to make such a long trip. If they quit paying tithing they could easily save $150 in three months. But that never occurred to them. They could quit paying building fund, fast offerings, Elder's Quorum dues and branch budget donations. But that never occurred to them either. Tithes and offerings were as much a part of the Lord's plan as the temple was. They would follow His plan. All of His plan.

It looked like another year would pass before they could be sealed as an eternal family. It was disappointing, but Bill and Myke were so glad just to know that the opportunity was open to them. They were used to working patiently toward the things they wanted. Setting up and following a savings plan was easy. Bill and Myke would do their part and trust the Lord to do His.

He did! And He did it on a very grand scale. Sometimes the blessing sent to answer the needs of one person involves so many other people that it is hard to realize it was meant primarily for the one. It should not be hard to understand, but, for some reason, it often is. Quickly acknowledged is the fact that Christ willingly suffered in Gethsemane for the sins of all—knowing that only a few would take advantage of His efforts in our behalf. Even more, He would gladly suffer for all in order to give an opportunity to only one. This is clearly understood. Why, then, is it so difficult in our daily lives to see the Lord's hand in large things for the benefit of one?

Malachi pointed out this inability to see a blessing from the Lord simply because so many people are involved in bringing it about when he talked of the Lord pouring out a blessing "that there shall not be room enough to receive it" (Malachi 3:10). For some, there is not room enough in their faith to receive—to understand—the magnitude of the Savior's care or the scope of His blessings.

The Masons, however, had enough faith. They felt awe at His workings while they were humbly cradled in the warmth of His care.

In the current circumstances, the Masons could not go to the temple, even though they were worthy and doing all that they could do. So the Lord changed the circumstances! He inspired the Navy to construct a new commissary building at the submarine base in Groton, Connecticut where the Masons shopped. Moving the large inventory would be very expensive, so prices were slashed. Myke remembers, "For the next three months the sales at the old commissary were unbelievable! Hamburger was thirteen cents a pound. Hot dogs were nine cents a package. We were able to feed our family on $30 a month instead of the usual $80. In three months we had exactly what we needed to make the trip to the temple. We've shopped at the commissary for fifty years now. Never before or since have we seen a sale. The Lord did that just for us!"

The whole family was so excited! But there was one more problem about the trip that concerned Myke and Bill. They wanted a harmonious spirit to be with them while they traveled. Their children, ages four, five and six, were good travelers, but this journey would stretch the little ones beyond their limits. This was a trial that could be endured. But it would be very nice if it could be lifted from them!

One day while trying to figure out how five people could comfortably spend several days and nights in the car, a full-blown idea suddenly filled Bill's mind. Grabbing his tools, he headed out to the Rambler. He pulled out the back seat, took a few measurements, assembled a little lumber, added a hinge here, a safety catch there, and presto! The back seat could be laid down flat! The children now had a play area and enough room to stretch out and go to sleep. The trip was looking better by the minute. Prayers of elation were offered that night by two relieved parents.

In the pre-dawn of December 16, the little ones were bundled into the car. Forty-four hours later their gray Rambler pulled into the parking lot beside the Salt Lake Temple. It was midnight. The tired little family slept in the car until the temple opened. On 19 December 1959 they were sealed together for time and all eternity.

They had another eternal blessing as well: a sure testimony of the law of tithes and offerings. Bill explains, "There are many competing ideas about how to best use money during our time on earth. Learning to handle it in the Lord's way is a necessary part of life. Putting complete faith and trust in a savings plan or a sale is a mistake. There is no retailer who can make a dime stretch farther than the Lord's Tithe 'N' Save." Confidently the Masons testify that after we have done all that we can for ourselves, the Lord steps in and does whatever else is needed.

London and Leather Wallets
Jane and Claus Goldner

Her parents met in post-war Palestine. Her father, a British soldier, was there helping to create the independent nation of Israel. Her mother, raised in Poland, was a Jewish immigrant whose family came to the Holy Land in the 1930's.

In 1947 the unlikely couple married, and they later moved back to England. Typical of a family with a military breadwinner, Jane Gildner and her mother and sisters frequently moved during the course of her growing-up years. The moves made it hard for her to feel a part of the communities they lived in. This situation was compounded by the fact that they were a non-traditional family—not only in ancestry, but in religious beliefs. Entirely tolerant of each other's personal beliefs, Jane's parents insisted that each of their children search out and decide for themselves which, if any, of the many churches on the face of the earth they wished to join.

For Jane, this was a challenge that she cherished. She had regularly prayed since she was a little child, and finding the church which to her was Christ's own was a continuous life priority. As a teenager she visited many churches. She looked into her parents' religions, the Church of England and the Jewish faith. "But," Jane says, "as motivated as I was to find a church to join, none of them felt right. I always felt so different—so left out by others, especially for not simply attending the Church of England. I discovered that even attending the same church over a period of time, I would hear different teachings, depending on who was preaching that week. I found it disillusioning!"

When Jane was fourteen, her maternal grandparents traveled from Israel to visit the family. She was fascinated by their value system, which was a direct reflection of their orthodox Jewish beliefs. But as drawn to their lifestyle as she was, it came down to one immutable point; she already had a firm testimony that Jesus was the Messiah. Such a belief would never be a part of her grandparents' religion; there was no way to reconcile the teachings of Judaism with that wondrous fact.

So Jane continued searching right through grammar school. In 1968, after graduation, she went to work at Barclay's Bank in London. Barclay's was one of a handful of centuries old banking institutions that flourished in the finance section of old London town. Prospective employees went through a rigid series of interviews and background checks before being hired. Jane was very proud, and justifiably so, the day she received word she could begin work as a teller.

Jane moved her few possessions from home into a "bed-sitter" (an apartment with the sitting room and bedroom all in one, and a small kitchen and bathroom) with a girl friend.

Bank customers came in a steady flow, Monday through Friday. However, she soon noted a special few who always came with deposits, requests for cash, and so forth, only on Mondays. For the most part they were young men dressed in suits with name tags identifying them as "elder" so-and-so. They sported Yank accents and big grins.

Jane soon learned they were missionaries for The Church of Jesus Christ of Latter-day Saints. One young man in particular always made a point of handing Jane, along with his deposit, a leaflet explaining some facet of the Mormon Church. Jane was intrigued. The young man, Elder David Wall—missionary and mission accountant—always thereafter maintained that he saw in the lovely blonde teller's glowing countenance a golden contact, and so it would prove.

After some weeks of being informally fed information on Christ's Church in this day and age, Jane had an opportunity to finish work early. She had faithfully read the pamphlets coming through her teller's window, and an overwhelming desire to know more had been born within her. With the bonus late-afternoon time, she decided to make a bee-line for the mission home. After finding the appropriate door, she asked for Elder Wall, and that very night had her first discussion on the gospel. In every succeeding session with the missionaries Jane's every question, saved up from a lifetime of query, was answered. "It was", she says, "like a GIANT puzzle coming together, piece by piece, with every question they answered."

Before the end of the discussions, Jane had committed to baptism. But the wondrous changes about to take place in Jane's life just began with the missionary discussions. One week before her baptism date, Jane met Claus Gildner, a fourth-generation Mormon from Germany, who was working in North London as a journeyman mechanic for Volkswagen. They began courting shortly thereafter.

Jane joined the Church and wasted no time in immersing herself in total Church activity. From the moment she learned of the law of tithing she conscientiously complied with it.

In the early spring of 1970, Jane and Claus became engaged to be married. The sealing date was set for July. They spent the intervening months carefully planning for their marriage, budgeting their spare earnings to cover the cost of the wedding and honeymoon. Claus owned a VW bug that generally worked quite well for getting the couple around; they decided to go on a low-cost, high-fun honeymoon by touring Europe via the bug and campgrounds along the way.

But the costs associated with everyday life, let alone the added burden of a wedding and dual receptions (in England and Munich for relatives and friends in both countries) rendered the couple all but broke. Nevertheless, the plans were all made and Jane's anticipation grew daily. But Murphy's Law reared its ugly head a few weeks before the big day in July. Their carefully laid plans were shattered by damage done to the VW in an accident. There was no money to fix the car. So much for a honeymoon!

As Jane and Claus discussed options to circumvent this rather large dose of bad fortune, Jane remembers suggesting they should still go ahead and pay their tithing first. She says, "The missionaries always taught me that if the law of tithing was obeyed in full that there would be blessings." So, as bleak as things looked for transportation for their honeymoon, they each turned in their tenth to the Lord. Jane recalls the surprise of the event which followed in these words:

"A few days later we decided to pay a visit to my aunt, who lived in a basement flat in the London suburb of Knightsbridge. She was a widow, and was staying with my parents when I was born, so we had always been close. I frequently went to spend an afternoon with her.

"As we descended the steps to her flat, we found a finely-grained leather wallet. We picked it up and examined the contents to determine who to return it to. But when we looked in it, it only contained one thing, and lots of that! It was so odd—this beautiful, expensive wallet had absolutely no identification in it, but instead, a great deal of cash!

"We turned it in to the local police station, and never thought about it again until we were duly notified that both the wallet and its contents were ours. No one had ever come to claim it!

"With this money we fixed our car in time for the wedding. It was great once again having reliable transportation. But more than that, our bishop offered to let us use his camper bus for our honeymoon. After the ceremony in the London Temple we drove to Switzerland where we camped right behind the Swiss Temple.

"Even though the return trip was rather exciting, (customs officials confiscated all of our wedding presents from the Munich reception when we returned to England) they did let us return the camper to the bishop!"

For Jane and Claus, the years since their marriage have been filled with incredible challenges as they have immigrated to the United States and raised a family (Carl, Spencer and Rienna). But when financially challenged, Jane recalls that long-ago moment of blind faith and the resulting blessings: "What I remarked to Claus those many years ago as we contemplated turning in our tithing or getting the car fixed still holds so very true. 'These things—the promises of the Lord when we are obedient to His commandments—really work!'"

Life Impacting

Scott Shakespeare

High School in Bountiful, Utah was all fun and games for Scott Shakespeare. Without wanting to boast, Scott felt he could honestly claim that he had reached the exalted rank of Senior without having had to learn anything life-impacting. A key to the art room let him slip away from the unwanted demands of class assignments and hall monitors. Scott spent his energy and appreciation on girls, good friends, and Grandma's Cookies.

In 1989 he appreciated only one girl, Kim. She was short, with dark hair, a great figure and terrific smile. Scott loved that smile. He bought her presents and took her out to eat several times a week just to see it.

But life needs balance, so when he wasn't with Kim, Scott could be found with Adam, Darron and Steve. They had been friends for so long that their camaraderie was bound with carefully constructed rituals and traditions. One such tradition involved nearly one-hundred dollars' worth of junk food, rented movies, sleepless nights and eating until they got sick. It was an honored tradition, a cherished memory.

There were other memorable moments from those years—like the day Scott proudly brought his SHOEI HR helmet home. It was uniquely styled, full-faced, and the inside looked like a car interior. For five months it had languished in Lay Away while Scott eagerly paid the $200 price. The day he brought it home was incredibly exciting. It made him wish he had a motorcycle to go with it. Eventually a Kawasaki 750 LTD made the helmet useful.

Impulse guided Scott's life. As the consequences occurred, he either faced them or hid from them, whichever he felt like doing at the moment. It was a comfortable way to live most of the time.

Then, in Scott's senior year, his family rediscovered the gospel. A new world opened up for him: new concepts, new rules, new influences, and new friends.

John Fairbanks was one of those influences. In the summer of 1989, John was called to serve a mission in Guatemala. He was the first person Scott knew personally who was going to serve a mission. Scott was so excited for him that he called everyone who even vaguely knew John to tell them about it. Delighted responses fed Scott's enthusiasm. He decided he wanted to be a part of something this exciting.

There was just one little hitch. Scott really didn't know much about the gospel! Although he and all his friends were LDS, they hadn't exactly been living in a way that would get a write-up in The *New Era*. No Sunday School or Primary lessons were in their minds. They were definitely starting from scratch!

It didn't take long to realize that there was only one sure way to learn what they wanted to know: read the scriptures. Amazed at the quirks and turns in life, Scott shook his head. Incredible as it seemed, he actually wanted to read and study a book! What would his friends think? Fortunately, they thought it was great and decided to make scripture reading a new tradition for their group.

After careful deliberation, they chose Mueller Park Canyon as their scripture-reading place. Food was a must in all of their traditions so, armed with their scriptures and an assortment of fire munchies (hot dogs, marshmallows, etc.), Scott, Darron, Adam and Steve drove to the canyon. In this peaceful setting, they read the scriptures, often sharing particular passages and discussing how they applied to teenagers in 1989.

Scott was thrilled to belong to something really good, something that didn't have its origin in a movie or a rock group. They retreated often to the canyon to pray and discuss gospel principles. John joined them once or twice before he left for Guatemala. While he was on his mission, John's family moved to Florida and Scott never saw him again, but his influence remained.

The more Scott learned about the gospel, the more he liked it. A transformation was taking place in each member of their group. They had been crude in their jokes and actions. That was losing its appeal. Now they talked about a direction for their lives and what their personal rules would be.

Feelings this rich, this deeply fulfilling, had to be shared. Scott wanted to share them as a missionary. It would be expensive, but he was working two jobs and had a small business of his own airbrushing designs on T-shirts. Surely, with three sources of income, he could earn enough for his share of mission expenses. He opened a checking account with the idea that he would just dump his paychecks in it one after the other and in no time at all he'd be in the mission field.

But he forgot about Kim. It was so fun to spend money on her. She was always so happy when he bought her something. And Scott enjoyed going out to dinner and a movie. Often. But he just knew there would be enough money for all his "needs." After all, he was going to start paying tithing. That would guarantee an endless flow of money, wouldn't it?

He had never paid tithing before, but he couldn't see how it would be a challenge. It was simple: dump the money in the checking account and write the first check to the Lord. Right? He was good at writing checks. What could be easier?

Maybe it would have been easier if he and Kim hadn't worked at the same place. Then it wouldn't have been so tempting to take his check and his girl and head out for fun at closing time. Sometimes his money was spent before he even thought about tithing. He seemed to be "catching up" a lot.

This was not working out like he had thought it would. Paying tithing was not giving him an endless flow of money and it was not easy, either. It was not that it was hard to pay—it wasn't—but it was very hard to think about paying! Now he had to have priorities. Even worse, he had to discipline himself and resist impulses he had always given in to before. Paying tithing was changing his lifestyle!

A niggling suspicion was born that the blessings of God's laws were most often natural consequences of living a certain way. Resisting impulses to spend left money to save. Tithing made him think about money in a new way. Perhaps money was provided by the Lord for the Lord's purposes, not for selfish wastefulness. It was time to get serious about tithing. Scott had to have proof of this principle in his own life before he could share his testimony of it to others, and time was running out. Only a few months remained before he was to report to the Missionary Training Center. Scriptural promises ran through his mind: " . . . when we obtain any blessing from God, it is by obedience to that law upon which it is predicated" (Doctrine and Covenants 130:21); "Return unto me, and I will return unto you . . . prove me now herewith, saith the Lord of hosts . . . " (Malachi 3:7, 10). Scott decided to live the law and watch for the blessings.

As soon as he started paying his tithing first, without fail, orders started coming in to his basement T-shirt business. Scott's little sister brought him his first big order. Her friend's father ordered some shirts to sell in his booth at a hunting convention. An old girlfriend brought another order. Little Caesar's was having a mud volleyball tournament between the Salt Lake and Bountiful stores. Scott was commissioned to airbrush the Bountiful store's team T-shirts. One hundred and fifty mauve T-shirts with a silhouette of a 1920's flapper went to Tooele County Health and Human Services for a women's conference.

The law of tithing was working! It hit him one day when he opened his mail and found a total of $600 in payments for jobs that had been sent to him. Yes, he had done the work. Yes, friends and family had referred him to these customers. But he'd had those same friends and family for many years and nothing like this had happened before. As Scott sat with the checks in his hand, a new understanding filled his mind: doors are opened through tithing.

That $600 was crucial. It opened the door to his mission. On September 5, 1990 Scott Shakespeare entered the door of the Missionary Training Center confident that he could teach the principle of tithing and testify of the great impact tithing can have in your life.

Found Funding
Mida and Phil Pedersen

That overcast, late spring day in the Pacific Northwest in May 1962 began as hundreds before it had, with Mida Pedersen packing her husband Phil's huge black lunchbox with three peanut butter and jelly sandwiches and various other snackables as he rushed to lace up his logging boots and leave home by 5 o'clock a.m. for the logging camp.

Mida bustled about the kitchen, busy with the lunch box, with baby Cindy Ann who invariably woke up with her parents, and with household concerns for the coming day. For the first time in their marriage she missed the opportunity to give Phil a kiss good-bye. It was an omission that would come back to haunt her by the end of the day.

From the moment Mida and Phil had met, five years earlier, at a dance in Longview, Washington, their relationship had been special. Mida was a high school senior while Phil worked fire watch in a look-out tower for the Forestry

Service. She went home after the dance and announced to her folks that she had met the man she would marry; "I just knew the first moment I laid eyes on him that I had known him before," she says. Phil came to Mida's home in the Elocohman Valley just a few days later. It was a week night, and her family was hosting the branch's mutual activities in their home. Within a few remarkable days, Phil was introduced not only to his future wife, but to the gospel! Five months later he joined the Church and in June 1958, they were married.

The fiscal realities of family life quickly induced Phil to leave the seasonal work of the Forestry Service and join a local logging crew. It was after all, the Pacific Northwest, and logging was a booming industry.

After one year in Longview, they moved back to Mida's old stomping ground, the forested hills of Cathlamet, Washington on the shores of the Elocohman River. In the early 1960's it was a fairly isolated community. Longview was one hour to the east, while metropolitan Portland, Oregon was over two hours' drive away. Mida kept herself more than busy caring for her brood and three-bedroom home. Her life was now full with husband, house and children—the oldest David, only three, twenty-month-old Cindy and five-month-old Kristina. The winter of '62 in western Washington had been a tempestuous time in their lives—their move from Longview to Cathlamet, working odd hours on renovating the old home, the freezing rains, and Mida suffering in January from staph pneumonia which caused the early arrival of Kristina. But May brought the sunshine of jonquils, johnny-jump-ups and kinder weather. Her life had settled into a hectic hum. As she explains, even though they were literally tucked away in the woods, "I had too much to do to take time to go crazy!"

There was always some concern in the back of the young couple's minds about the potential for a logging accident, but it was nothing that they dwelt on. They were confident that Phil's conservative, safety-conscious approach to working in the woods ensured his continued health and a steady income for the family. He usually worked as a choker setter, placing immense steel cables around the logs.

However, on that particular May day he was "whistle punking"; signalling by means of coded whistle calls to the cat operators when the cable was placed. The crew had just finished lunch and was starting the logging operations again. Phil was standing to the side of the log pile, with the cat at one end of his vision and the choker setter at the other, when it happened. A massive one-and-one-half-inch cable, just being wrenched up by the cat, caught a snag and jerked loose to whip across the clearing and smash with deadly force into Phil's face. If it had been just one eighth of an inch higher or lower it would have killed him. As it was, it broke both of his jaws, split open the roof of his mouth, damaged his sinuses, one eye socket and his hearing. Incredibly, it left his nose intact!

By the time representatives of the logging outfit had located Mida where she was visiting at her mother's, Phil was in the hospital. The projected six-week stay lasted only three. But, recovering from the logging accident was the least of the trials the little family would face. Not surprisingly, Phil decided logging was not his profession of choice.

With the help of local college career counselors, Phil entered college to work on a degree in instrument technology. He would be a full time student for the next three years.

He would also continue working full-time to support his growing family. He went to classes during the day, then worked nights "pulling green chain" (hauling newly cut lumber off the cutting belts) at a Longview saw mill.

Weekends he put in time as a counselor in the elder's quorum presidency. The Pedersens moved back to Longview to shorten the commute time for Phil, but Mida and the children still had only one hour a day with their husband and father.

No doubt about it, times were tough. Mida remembers one morning in particular when she snuck her husband's only pair of shoes—full of more holes than a sieve—to the garbage truck so that he would be forced to buy a new pair. But though finances were tight, they were young, once again healthy, and knew where they were headed. When Phil felt like throwing in the towel, Mida would announce that she would rather have "holy" shoes for a short time than for the rest of their lives.

In Phil's final year of school, Christmas came at an unusually tight time for the not-so-little family. Child number four was now on the way. Even though Phil got paid every other week, it just seemed about seven days too long a wait. That December day Mida sat down to pay the bills, a solitary job since Phil was doing double duty away from home. Her eyes rested on the amount due for tithing. Her mind went rapidly over the small list of presents yet to be purchased for the children; then, resolutely, she picked up the pen and wrote out the check to The Church of Jesus Christ of Latter-day Saints. No, never could she betray her trust in the Lord, nor His in her. That Sunday she handed in the check to the bishop, thinking to herself, "I just hope payday comes quicker than I think it will!"

A few days later, as she scurried about the kitchen, putting away just-washed dishes, she reached high to place some plates on an upper shelf in the spice cabinet. Oddly, she felt something with the tips of her fingers in a cereal bowl. Mida pulled the bowl down, and discovered a twenty dollar bill—the equivalent in 1996 monies of over ninety-five dollars! Astounded, she immediately queried family members and friends about her unexpected find. No one could (or would) account for the mysterious appearance of the money.

And, Mida says quite frankly, she did not carry out an extensive search for the source of the money—it was quickly put to good use to meet the family's Christmas-time needs. She still has no idea where that twenty dollar bill came from, nor why she felt the need to feel inside the cereal bowl before placing the stack of clean dishes on the high shelf; but she has remained steadfast in her belief that no matter how tough times get, the Lord is watching over her family. After all, even Phil's logging accident was just that—an accident, not a tragedy. His life was spared by a miniscule one eighth of an inch, and the family's needs always somehow met in the ensuing years. In Mida Pedersen's mind, two things she will never forgo are paying tithing and kissing her husband goodbye in the morning!

Single, But Never Alone

Paulette Youngberg

Divorce was a wrenching experience. Even though she'd seen it coming, knew it was for the best, and yearned for the peace her new living situation would bring, it was extremely painful. Separating two lives that were entwined in the thousand-and-one details of daily routine presented constant, unpleasant surprises. And the process of dissolution seemed to go on forever.

No longer restrained by hopes for the future, the frustrations and disappointments of many years surged to the surface. The days seemed endless, and Paulette Youngberg's pain seemed endurable only through earnest prayer. The words of a hymn took on new meaning as she sent her appeals heavenward so many times each day; "Prayer is the Christian's vital breath, The Christian's native air . . . " (*Hymns*, #145) and in that environment, Paulette's freedom came without anger, bitterness or resentment.

But with limited formal education, she was somewhat concerned about finding a good job; the job market wasn't an ideal place for the untrained. Yet it wasn't the need to support her little family that caused her the greatest worry. She had always worked to help provide for her family's needs. Being responsible for paying bills was old hat. And long ago, Paulette had learned that the best way to make a dollar stretch was to pay an honest tithe. No, she wasn't worried about making ends meet. The Lord would take care of that. It was the challenge of wisely weighing all her life options, then making the decisions alone, that jump-started her heart. Her rioting pulse was controlled only when she reminded herself to take life one step at a time and to discuss each choice with the Lord.

One of the giant steps she took in the fall of 1981 was to move from the west coast back to her childhood home. Back in Ohio, the rich, warm, autumn-toned leaves comfortably rustling in strong, old trees stirred happy memories of long-forgotten security. The thick grass was a soft cushion between Paulette and the hard, rocky world from which it sprang, and she really needed a cushion from the world right then. In no time at all Paulette and thirteen-year-old Bobby Jean had settled into a small trailer that quickly became home. The next step was to find work.

Paulette wasn't worried about her ability to hold a job, but she was concerned about finding one. Job opportunities were scarce in the little town of Columbus Grove. However, she had a partner in the job search that was out of this world—literally. If she did her part, He would do His. To the best of her ability, she had always kept her part of the covenants she made. She had paid her tithing even when no one else in the family approved. This gave her complete confidence that the needed blessings would come. It was just a little nerve-wracking waiting for them.

But soon Paulette was working weekday afternoons from three to seven o'clock as a custodian in the Columbus Grove School District. She made the twelve mile round-trip every day in her trusty Chevy Vega, and every day she was grateful for an economical car. It soon became apparent, however, that even for the Vega there wasn't going to be enough money for gas. What was she going to do now? Paulette saw only one possible solution. She could take it from her tithing money. It was such a pitifully little amount. Would it *really* matter? After all, the Lord actually sent the job, didn't He?

She felt awful as soon as she thought about using her tithing that way. Of course it mattered! The Lord sent the job and He would send a way for her to get there every day. Paulette paid her tithing. Knowing that she couldn't manufacture more money or create circumstances for extra earnings or make a tank of gas last longer, she put her faith in the Lord and gave Him complete control of her finances. There was no one else to turn to. She had done all that she could do.

A few days later Paulette's neighbor, Chung Hee, asked if Paulette could give her a ride to the employment office every other week. Chung Hee didn't have her driver's license yet and sixteen miles was too far to walk. She would be happy to pay Paulette for her trouble.

Astounded at her good fortune, Paulette did a little quick math. The amount Chung Hee offered, minus tithing, equaled the amount needed for gas to get to work! Overwhelming gratitude filled her heart as she sank to her knees and thanked Heavenly Father.

By keeping the law of tithing, Paulette accepted the Lord as her partner. No matter what options had to be found or what decision had to be made, He was there for her. A feeling of great security and peace engulfed her as she realized that although she was single, she was never alone.

The Phone Rang as They Prayed
Jean and Duane Crowther

They met at BYU in the fall of 1957. Jean Decker was in her third year, working on a degree with an Elementary Education major and a Music minor. Duane Crowther, returning to the Y after a two-and-one-half-year mission in Central America, was beginning his junior year in Music Education.

Mary, Jean's sister, was their connecting link. She had been the accompanist for a choir Duane had directed just before his mission. Jean was a silent observer as Duane and Mary renewed their friendship in a brief sidewalk encounter, early in the quarter. But several days later, when Duane came into the Reserve Library where Jean worked, they became aware of each other. Attraction quickly blossomed into romance, and they were married in the Arizona Temple just five months later.

Both Jean and Duane came from strong LDS families—families which had several lines of genealogical roots reaching back to the early days of the gospel's restoration. Most of their great grandparents crossed the plains to Utah during the pioneer era before the railroad arrived. Jean grew up just a few houses from the Arizona Temple and, as a young girl, was often called to that sacred structure to do baptisms for the dead. Duane was raised in Arlington, Virginia. His father, after serving in the Eastern States Mission, went back east from Colorado to attend George Washington University, and stayed on in Washington, D.C. to work for the United States government.

Growing up in modest homes from their early childhood on, both Jean and Duane had learned and lived the law of tithing. As life-long full tithe payers, they had never been challenged by that law. The first real tests of their tithing obedience were to come in their first two years of marriage as they struggled to finish school and begin their family.

When they first married, they were both carrying heavy class schedules and working student-level half-time jobs. Both were going to school full-time, and both were student teaching every quarter. Duane had a scholarship, but finances were extremely tight. Like many student newlyweds, they were busy and happy and, oh so poor.

The couple shared a strong mutual interest in music. Duane played alto sax in the BYU Concert Band. Jean played viola in the BYU Orchestra. Both played several instruments and had wide musical interests. Duane was student conductor for the University Chorale. On an extra-curricular level he was playing in one of the large off-campus dance bands and was singing in the ROTC Chorus.

As the fall quarter of 1958 began, Duane and Jean decided to organize a small dance band—a five-piece "combo"—to provide another source of much-needed extra income.

The Phone Rang as They Prayed

Duane would play alto and tenor sax and Jean would play the string bass. They added a piano and drums. Jean's sister, Carolyn, was recruited to play trumpet and violin. Rehearsals were undertaken in earnest. By November they scheduled their first dance.

They squeezed through Christmas, but money remained really tight. Jean's half-time job in the Reserve Library was paying for the rent. Duane's four-o'clock-in-the-morning campus custodian job helped pay other bills. In their plan, the dance band jobs were needed to provide for a rather vital budgetary item, the groceries!

During Winter Quarter, from January through March, 1959, Duane was student teaching each day fifteen miles to the north in Pleasant Grove. He had enrolled in the Church Education System's seminary training program so he was teaching half-days in both the Seminary and music programs. The further daily travel created more expenses for gas and car maintenance. Also, they were expecting their first child; the extra medical bills stretched their inflexible budget beyond the snapping point. As January turned into February, the financial pressure mounted. There just wasn't enough money!

Their fledgling "combo" played a couple of dances in early February, which generated some much-needed extra income, but by late February, their finances hit bottom. One Friday night, the kitchen shelves were just about empty, and it was still another week before payday. In desperation, Duane and Jean knelt in prayer, asking for guidance and help, and seeking some source of income to get them through the coming week. They reminded Heavenly Father that their tithing had been paid, and they put themselves in His hands.

While they were still pouring out their hearts in prayer, their telephone rang. The anxious caller said, "Our club has a dance slated for tonight, and we've just discovered a scheduling mix-up with our dance band. We have no band! We're desperate!! Can your group come and play for us?"

Duane quickly made calls to the band members (all of whom were available) and The Cavaliers played the dance to an appreciative audience. The grateful young couple bought groceries the following day. The Crowthers marveled at how quickly their prayer was answered, and they quietly acknowledged their private "miracle" as their emergency needs were met.

But further blessings were still in store for them. Half a week later, on March 5th, the seminary coordinator for Duane's student teaching told him the seminary officials wanted him to stop by the central office that day. When Duane went in, he was informed that a teacher at Bountiful High School had given notice that he was leaving the Seminary program immediately to take a job at LDS Hospital. Duane had been selected, from all the candidates in the seminary program, to be offered his position. They asked him to drop out of school and begin teaching full time at the Bountiful High Seminary for the rest of the school year. They offered him one-third of the regular beginning seminary teacher's annual contract: $1,366 to teach the last three months of school! Four days later, on March 9th, he was on the job, teaching 210 students a day. It was a real baptism by fire in the teaching profession, complete with a one-and-one-half hour commute each way, but their financial problems were alleviated for the next several months and they were able to pay the medical expenses for the birth of their first son.

Duane and Jean enjoyed a double graduation in their respective fields from BYU in August 1959. The ink on the degrees was barely dry before they were discussing the possibility of staying another year in Provo. By doing so, Duane could finish a Master's degree by the following August. After hours of prayer, they made the decision to stay and pursue the Master's degree—a degree in the Department of Religious Instruction with an Old Testament major and a New Testament minor.

Jean had been offered a full-time position as Reserve Librarian and Duane had obtained work instructing an early-morning Seminary class at Lehi High School. The dance band, which had been expanded into a twelve-piece group, soon had several dances scheduled for the school year. The now-experienced budgeters made up a monthly income/expense projection and dived into the new school year.

It was a good year, with many happy times, but every penny still had to be counted. They had a small but comfortable basement apartment. The Crowthers hired a part-time baby sitter for the baby, Don, while Jean was working during the day. They found a dear, older woman to care for him during their dance band jobs. Child care expenses ate up all of their available cash.

They lived frugally and conscientiously paid their tithing. Money for anything beyond the essentials was scarce.

Then they had another experience which showed them that God was aware of their needs and was watching over them. One early spring day in 1960, Jean came home from work to find a visitor waiting. Duane's uncle, Ralph Swofford, had stopped "to meet his new niece" as part of a business trip between his home in El Paso, Texas and

Nevada. He was traveling with his pet dog, a huge black Labrador, as his companion. Duane wasn't there at the time, but Uncle Ralph introduced himself and Jean invited him in. This was the first time Jean had met any members of Duane's mother's family and, at first, she felt a little bit uncomfortable. (Even if Duane had been at home when Uncle Ralph arrived, he would have been little help to Jean—he'd only met him a few times in his early youth.) But Jean soon overcame her concern and invited Uncle Ralph to supper.

Jean and Duane don't remember just what was served for supper that night—it must have been a frugal menu because of the circumstances of their life. But Uncle Ralph was complimentary and they had a good visit. The dog even enjoyed the leftovers before Ralph said good-bye and departed for his motel. Uncle Ralph indicated that he planned an early start the next morning so as to reach his destination in Nevada before nightfall.

The next day Jean came home from work unexpectedly during her lunch hour. She was startled to find Uncle Ralph's car parked in the driveway. She hurried in the door, worried that something was the matter. She surprised Uncle Ralph, who was coming up the stairs from the apartment with his hands full of empty boxes. He mumbled something about the landlord letting him in. He said that he'd bought a wedding present for them, but he couldn't stay because he had to get on his way immediately.

Jean wished him farewell and thanked him for the unknown gift, then she went downstairs. There she found her kitchen counters and table completely covered with cans and boxes of food of all kinds. There were large bags of flour and sugar, cases of fruits and vegetables, and large quantities of cleaning supplies and paper goods. Opening the refrigerator, she found it completely full of fresh vegetables, fruits, dairy foods and meats—many things she'd never been able to afford to buy in their year-and-a-half of marriage. There was so much food that she was overwhelmed and burst into tears. This was more than a wedding gift. Uncle Ralph had provided them with food enough to last for several months!

As she observed the great abundance of food and supplies, Brother Wright, their landlord, knocked on the door. He told her that their visitor had observed their frugal standard of living and had quietly checked out their kitchen cupboards the night before. Ralph had canceled his sales meetings in Nevada and spent the whole morning shopping at the grocery store. He told Brother Wright that he hadn't had that much fun in years, and planned to leave everything as a surprise.

The food left that beautiful spring day fed the Crowther family for many weeks. The immediate relief from having to spend money for groceries allowed overdue bills to be paid. They sent heartfelt letters of thanks to Uncle Ralph, but he never acknowledged his "good deed" nor replied concerning it.

Although the gift of food from their Uncle Ralph was not as direct a result from prayer and paying tithing as the dance job blessing, Jean and Duane Crowther are convinced that God's loving kindness was manifested in both incidents. Other blessings occurred during those student years that could be accounted for as being a result of careful observance of keeping the commandments. And the same type of quiet, ongoing blessings continue in their lives to this day as they endeavor to remain faithful to all that the Lord asks of them.

Giving Thanks
Cheryl and John Palmers

A wise man once observed, "Yes, risk-taking is inherently failure-prone. Otherwise, it would be called sure-thing-taking."

The early 90's was a period of risk-taking both for John and Cheryl Palmers and for their extended families. Cheryl's parents were high school sweethearts who grew up together in Klamath Falls, Oregon, and had spent adulthood pursuing the dream of that just-perfect job. After receiving a Ph.D. from BYU, Cheryl's father had worked in a number of positions in computer technology at west-coast based universities. By 1993 the family made a huge career jump—both strategy-wise and geographically—by becoming partners in a Maryland computer consulting firm. Money proved tight as they embarked on the new venture.

John's family, long-time Californians, still lived in Turlock, California, where they had raised their children. John had been only seven when the missionaries had come to their door, and the family had immediately embraced the gospel message. Now his family was dealing financially with his dad's retirement from the power company. Their sole income came from his mom, who still worked teaching school.

With jobs scarcer than hen's teeth, the Palmers had risked sticking it out with Pizza Hut. John had begun work for the restaurant as a part-time delivery boy, but within a dizzying eighteen months had moved up to manager. His income had taken commensurate leaps along the way, and the family had moved out of the cockroach-ridden one-bedroom apartment of their early days of marriage into a darling little house with garage and yard, trees and flowers. It was situated right next to John's grandmother's home. Both John and Cheryl had stake callings as Young Men's and Young Women's secretary, respectively. They loved the ward they were in, and basked in the healthy growth of their two little children. Life was downright rosy.

But out of the proverbial clear blue, within the course of a few days, John unexpectedly lost his job and the little family was thrown into financial turmoil. After a month of floundering in the local economy looking for more work, John and Cheryl called on help from their families. Neither set of parents was in a position to provide monetary relief, but John's brother opened his Redding, California home to them. Remarkably, John quickly found full-time work in Redding, but it provided only half the income of the restaurant job. The little family continued to struggle financially, falling behind in bills as Cheryl's health problems resurfaced in the form of diabetes. The condition spiraled out of control in November of 1994, just before Thanksgiving, when precious monies went for medicine and testing.

They were living, Cheryl says, "On next to nothing. The cupboards were literally bare. It was real apparent that we weren't going to have a Thanksgiving. And what little bit of money we had for tithing was difficult to give up. When the choice is, 'do I buy food for the children or pay the Lord?', it isn't always easy to take that step of faith."

Their pay check came, and they deliberated whether to postpone paying tithing in order to buy food. But back in those challenging days when John was delivering pizza part-time, they had learned to "return unto the Lord" first. Past experience, and the fact that John had a couple of weeks earlier taught the elder's quorum a lesson on paying tithing, in which a quote from President Kimball explained that the Lord was our most important Debtor and that our first obligation should always be to Him. It put the kitchen cupboard's barren condition into an eternal perspective. Without, well, *much* doubt, they knew what their first priority was. They decided to once again trust in the Lord.

On the Friday before Thanksgiving, Cheryl wrote out the check for tithing. It was sitting on the kitchen counter for Sunday delivery when she got a notice from the bank that they had been charged a twelve dollar overdraft fee. To this day, Cheryl cannot understand where they went wrong in their bookkeeping, but the fact remained that they knew they could not turn in the tithing check.

That Sunday morning, Cheryl knelt down next to her bed and poured her heart out to her Father in Heaven. "Father," she pleaded, "we keep trying to do the right thing, but obstacles keep coming up. Please help me to know what to do." With a worried heart, she rose from her bedside and returned to the many chores associated with getting two active little children ready for Church.

A few minutes after leaving her room, someone knocked at the front door. Cheryl could not imagine who would be calling so early on a Sunday morning. But, if she was just curious before opening the door, she was more than astonished to find a Federal Express representative on the porch. The polite young man handed her a special delivery packet. Puzzled by such a delivery, especially on a Sunday morning, Cheryl handled the cardboard envelope suspiciously. Finally, she tore the serrated strip across the top and, much to her amazement, pulled out a fifty dollar check from her sister, a student at the "Y". Attached to the check was a note explaining, "I just had a feeling that you needed this more than me." The tithing check was duly turned in to the bishopric that same morning!

Another day, and sixty more unexpected dollars came to them from a complete stranger. Then another fifty dollar check arrived in the mail from Cheryl's parents. John's new boss gave them a turkey for Thanksgiving, and with the unexpected funding they had a glorious holiday feast.

No matter how dire conditions appear to be, the Palmers have committed themselves to giving thanks first to the Lord, both in prayer and through the paying of tithes. Since that moment of truth at Thanksgiving, they first and foremost pay off their debt to the Lord. In return, they have since always had enough to cover the bills, including a little extra money left over, and somehow things just always work out. "In fact," they say, "we are at long last getting ahead!"

Cheryl concludes, "We were challenged; the Lord took us right to the edge of our faith, and then we reached out and now have a firm full-steam-ahead testimony of the principle of tithing and the blessings we get from consistently being obedient to it."

THE PROMPTING

Christine and Curtis Jasper

After nine months with only $200 income, it was no wonder that Curtis Jasper spent most of the five-and-a-half-hour drive from southeastern Washington back home to western Oregon trying to figure out how to break the news to his wife that he still felt that they should "stay the course" with their new job.

For years the couple had experienced a steady and more-than-adequate income as Curtis worked as a doctor of naturopathic medicine. But as time went on, and the family grew to seven children (Tara, Scooter [Patricia] Alyssa, Carstens, Curtis, Bear [Terry] and Jared) with child number eight on the way, Curtis and Christine both longed for a career that would allow Curtis adequate time on the home front.

In 1988 he started looking in earnest for just such a career change. At first it seemed appropriate that he should accept a position as a pharmaceuticals representative; several such companies were vigorously pursuing him for that purpose. His medical training made him a natural for their company needs. It was an awfully tempting route to take. Numerous such companies promised him not just sizable, steady pay, but to furnish the family with a car at no cost to them, and one hundred percent free medical and dental coverage.

The trade-off, though, as Curtis saw it, was no improvement on the amount of time he could spend at home; during every month he would have to travel from six to ten days out of the area. Nope, when he prayed about it, it just was not the answer, no matter how enticing the offers.

During the job search, Curtis had a chance to visit the Tri-Cities area of southern Washington. There he stayed with his sister's father-in-law. The old family friend had recently started with Xerox Corporation as a sales representative, working strictly eight-to-five, and with minimal travel time involved. Home every night, he had immediately started earning, as Curtis describes it, "a LOT of money!"

In spite of the straight-commission-only nature of the job, and so very little security in terms of regular income, Curtis felt that this was the opportunity he and Christine had been looking for. The company had an opening for a rep in the Walla Walla Valley, just forty-five minutes from the Tri-Cities.

This time, when the family made the job a matter of prayer, the Spirit shouted confirmation. Curtis started work for Xerox with two restrictions: one for the company—he would only start after the birth of his newest child (due the end of January, 1989), the other from his wife—to make the traumatic move of family from their long-time Willamette Valley home to the Walla Walla Valley only after the job had proved itself financially.

True to his word, Curtis started the job immediately after the birth of his last daughter, Jacinda, the end of January. True to his wife's desires, he boarded with family in the Tri-Cities, making the commute to Walla Walla daily. On weekends he traveled back to Salem, Oregon to spend time with Christine and the children. It was a beautiful drive along the spectacular Columbia River Gorge, but as the weeks stretched into months of this grueling routine, it sure grew old!

January quickly fled into February with not a single sale in Curtis's first month. This was a surprising first for the company, as nigh unto every new rep experienced some sort of sale—no matter how small—at some point in his first few weeks of employment. March and April followed discouragingly on the heels of the winter months, with absolutely no sales whatsoever. Curtis was beginning to wonder mightily at the prompting that this was the right job path for him and his family. Christine began to worry what they would do to survive once they had gone through their rapidly dwindling savings.

In May Curtis finally received a $200 commission, not because of any sale he had made, but because of the kindness of another sales rep who graciously handed over an already pocketed sale to the struggling Walla Walla rep.

The summer months continued in the same discouraging vein. It mattered not how hard he worked; no sales were forthcoming. Curtis's weeks were following an unvarying scenario: go to the Lord daily in prayer, receive confirmation that he was doing the right thing for his family, and then not get a single sale. Spend the weekends with an ever-more-worried Christine, both husband and wife trying to second guess the Lord. But, Curtis says, "It was always the same answer; I would doubt the wisdom of our decision to go with Xerox, but the Spirit would strongly whisper to us that 'this is the right thing to do'."

So, they hung in there. At the end of September, a miracle final occurred. As Curtis was driving down Rose Street in the heart of the Walla Walla business sector on his way to an appointment with the local college, the thought entered his mind to stop at the next nondescript building on his left. He found that a rather strange thought to pop into his head from nowhere, and so he ignored it. One block past the building, the prompting came again, so forcefully "that it might as well have been an audible voice," Curtis remembers. "It was a powerful prompting, and as it had now come twice, I decided to listen to it." He quickly turned around in the next available parking lot, returning to the building that he had, frankly, never even noticed before. The sign over the entrance marked it as the U. S. Department of Agriculture/Forest Service offices.

With nothing to lose, and feeling slightly silly, Curtis approached the receptionist and explained that he was with the Xerox Corporation. Not missing a beat, the young women answered "Oh, you must have an appointment with Marilyn." Nodding his head noncommittally, he followed the receptionist to Marilyn's office, who was indeed awaiting the arrival of a sales rep! She was in the process of soliciting proposals from various companies for purchase of a large copy machine, and assumed that Xerox was one of those that had received such a request. It wasn't. Nevertheless, Curtis walked out of her office with a request to bring in a demo machine the next morning. Twenty-four hours after his prompting, he made his first bona fide sale, earning him an $800 commission.

Back on the home front, Curtis and Christine made another important decision on this, the first earned income in nine long, lean months. The couple discussed postponing paying tithing until the end of the year, or immediately returning to the Lord His portion. Curtis felt strongly that they should "pay as we go along, no matter how difficult the circumstances. That really is the test isn't it? To be up front with the Lord when times are tough, not just when they are easy." And so they did. A tithing check was turned in the following Sunday.

In the coming seven weeks, Curtis went from one sale in nine months to an astounding forty machine sales tally, earning the family in a two-month period his original projected sales quota for the entire previous year! Did the family attribute it to their honest and up-front payment of tithes? You bet!

Since that year of trial, the Jasper's income from the Xerox job has more than met any type of forecasting they could ever have dreamed. And, unlike any of the pharmaceutical jobs, Curtis has the family time he had always yearned for. He also has had the opportunity to share several of what he considers his true talents, teaching and speaking: he has served for six years as a Seminary teacher for the Church, and also served as a high counselor and in several other positions. He even has time to coach a Little League baseball team (that, by the way, won its last game twenty-to-one!). All of these are activities that were impossible when he was working as a doctor.

On reminiscing on the lessons learned that undeniably hard year, Curtis says, "We learned not just the importance of putting the Lord first so that we could reap the blessings of tithing, but as a family we learned to trust in the Lord. We now understand that even though one job may—on paper—look a lot more secure, it is the Spirit speaking to us in our hearts that is the important thing to rely on. The Lord does not necessarily make it easy for us to follow His will, but He gives us a chance to prove our faith, and at the same time learn great lessons in trust and obedience. Our faith really grew from this experience. Just like a body muscle, having to exercise our faith regularly over a lengthy period of time resulted in a permanent strengthening of it. Only by consistently exercising it did we reap sizable and eternal benefits as a family."

No Laughing Matter
Jenny Hasty

The crisp autumn air rustled with the sounds of thousands of students arriving for the 1992 school year at Utah State University. Greetings and meetings echoed on the hillside as old friends reunited and new friends got acquainted. Friendships formed quickly for one new freshman with a bright smile and sunshine in her laugh; Jenny Hasty had brought her energy and optimism to college. Everything was wonderful in those first few days on campus, until registration!

Stunned, Jenny stared at the registration slip. Only one class was listed; German. All of the other classes had been dropped—canceled for lack of payment. She shook her head. This was a mistake. For nine months she had been filling out forms and meeting deadlines. Notification of a grant that covered her expenses had arrived a long time ago. Realizing that there was just some little glitch in the system that could be cleared up in a snap, she shook her head and with a rueful smile on her lips, bounced up the stairs to the Financial Aid Office.

Approaching the counter with confidence, Jenny began explaining the problem to a busy and unsympathetic clerk. The clerk began to bristle. A determinedly cheerful smile accompanied Jenny's evenly stressed words, "Well, I know I sent all the forms here in time."

Openly hostile now, the clerk yelled, "There is no possible way I could have lost your papers!" Her loud voice startled Jenny and carried throughout the room. People were looking—some with curiosity, some with embarrassment. Panic swelled inside as further attempts to resolve the problem were rebuffed.

No financial aid meant no place to stay, no food to eat and no classes to attend. The bureaucracy of higher education was new and very baffling to Jenny. She had no idea what to do. It looked like the only course of action open was to return home. This was a devastating blow, and Jenny began to cry.

She hated crying, she felt so stupid. She was always disgusted when people cried over things, but she couldn't help it. This problem was beyond her ability to solve. For the first time in her life she felt totally alone and very small. She needed help in a big way. Knowing that the most powerful friend a person could have was her Father in heaven, she turned to Him.

Jenny had always prayed. She knew her prayers would be answered. She also knew that blessings were based on obedience to their accompanying laws. Vaguely recalling that temporal care was connected to the law of tithes and offerings, she was suddenly very glad that she'd always paid her tithing. Of course, she'd done it without really thinking about it. It was just one of the things good girls do, so she did it. She'd never really considered the blessings she could claim, but she was considering them now.

She decided the next step was to return to the Registrar's Office and find a contact person—someone who had the power to hold those classes for her until this mess got straightened out. Jenny was directed to a Mrs. Poulson. After carefully listening to Jenny's dilemma, Mrs. Poulson agreed to hold the classes and even promised to make a phone call or two. With a wink she admitted that sometimes things got a little crazy the first couple days of a semester. Chalk one up for prayer!

Grateful, Jenny returned to her dorm. She settled into the Valley View Towers very quickly. It had already become her home and she was determined to stay; surely she could hang on for a few more days, if she just took things one day at a time.

Unfortunately, she had brought very little cash with her. Without any financial aid, there was no student I. D. card and therefore no access to the campus food service, and it had been two days since she'd eaten.

The next morning a very hungry, very nervous, very hopeful freshman returned to the Financial Aid Office. The still-nasty clerk looked up as Jenny entered and announced "Oh, there's the girl that cried." Jenny was unprepared for such an unprofessional assault. The clerk still insisted that no paperwork had been misplaced and refused to serve Jenny.

For six days Jenny made phone calls and visited every office she could think of in an effort to find the lost confirmation of her financial aid. Her friends knew she wasn't eating because she was getting crabby, "Come on, Jen," they would urge, "let's go to the cafeteria."

"O.K. Right. That's a good joke," Jenny recalls responding.

Finally, on the sixth day, she persuaded Mrs. Poulson to make a personal visit to the Financial Aid Office. It would shortly prove the right thing to do.

In a few hours Jenny was holding her student I. D. (with its food service code) and a full registration slip. The Lord had blessed her and Jenny was ecstatic. Clutching her prize, she headed for The Hub, one of the nicer restaurants on campus. This victory could not be commemorated by just a cafeteria meal!

Surrounded by friends, Jenny celebrated her deliverance with a big, thick ham and cheese sandwich and a side order of rice. Not a really good choice diet-wise, but it was hot and she ate *a lot*.

Her problem wasn't completely solved, but her naturally buoyant nature reasserted itself after such a scrumptious meal. Now she could think clearly about the rest of her dilemma. Even though tuition, room and board could be checked off the top of the list, additional income was now very necessary. Jenny presented her needs to the Lord: (1) an immediate infusion of cash to cover supplies for her classes and to get her laundry done, (2) a part-time job to enable her to continue to do her laundry, buy shampoo and all the other things that were needed for functional living, and (3) just a reminder that the situation was becoming critical!

Feeling certain that a solution was close by, Jenny realized that it wasn't likely to come find her in the dorm, so she pulled on a casual outfit and went out looking. Where there were people, there was opportunity. Besides, the first big dance of the school year was to follow some comedy routines in the outdoor recreation arena known as the "Quad" that night. Armed with her new student I. D. card, Jenny didn't have to miss any more activities—and she wasn't about to.

A stage was set up in the Quad for an audience participation game called, "You Laugh, You Lose." Anyone who wanted to could write his or her name on a piece of paper and put it in a big barrel. If your name was chosen, you got to go up on stage and try not to laugh. A straight face meant cold, hard cash. Each space on a big spinning wheel represented a different dollar amount. There was even a double or nothing space. A big smile covered Jenny's face as she placed her name in the barrel and prayed for her chance on stage.

Jenny didn't hesitate when her name was called. She jumped up on the stage and sat in the contestants' row of chairs. Each spin of the wheel brought an onslaught of outrageously dressed comedians doing very clever, very silly things, but Jenny remained straight-faced.

When the wheel came to rest on double or nothing, several contestants took their winnings and returned to their seats. Jenny decided to take the risk. She needed the money very badly.

At any other time, the dance of the mustached man dressed in a tutu would have been hilarious. Landing in front of Jenny, he held a cut-out of a grandma's face to his own and minced up to Jenny. He bent down, and crackled in an ancient voice, "Tell me that you love my chili!"

With six hungry days still vivid in her mind, Jenny stared into his eyes, and without a trace of a smile, replied, "I LOVE your chili." The crowd cheered and Jenny left the stage with sixty dollars. That was just enough to buy supplies for her classes and to pay her tithing.

She *had* to buy the class supplies, but the "extra" six dollars created an unexpected struggle. Being without funds was an experience she never wanted to have again. Although she had applied everywhere she could think of for a job, nothing had come of it so far. Part of her wanted to hang on to that six dollars for security, and part of her wanted to use it to do her laundry.

Memories of the last week filled her mind. At first she had felt so alone, but not any more. For the first time, she was certain that God was aware of her needs. It was comforting to know she was being watched over by someone so capable. The six dollars belonged to Him, and it was suddenly a completely inadequate return for all His care. Jenny was learning that the only true security comes through obedience to God's laws. With a glad and grateful heart, she paid her tithing. She could do her laundry in the bathroom sink.

A few days later a friend, Jennifer Morgan, had exciting news for Jenny. A local fabric store was hiring, but they had not advertised yet. Jenny was there in a flash. It took a couple of agonizing days, but finally the phone call came; "Do you still want a job?"

"Yes!" was her emphatic response. Jenny was now assured of an adequate income to meet her needs for the semester. She was also deeply assured of her Heavenly Father's care.

The law of tithing had always been one of the things Jenny did "just because." It had no real meaning for her. She thought it was mostly to help other people. Now she knows better. She now laughs with delight for the blessings tithing brings into her life.

We Couldn't Go Just Part Way
Golda and Neil Bishop

Seventy-one-year-young Brother Bishop, a high counselor in the Cedar City, Utah Stake of The Church of Jesus Christ of Latter-day Saints, is not reluctant to volunteer that his life example during much of his life was anything but perfect. Yet, through the many years of inactivity, he and his life companion, Golda, always felt deep inside that one day they would get their lives straightened around.

Neil Bishop was born in 1924 in Delta, Utah of pioneer stock, the last of seven children. He is frank to say that his mother was the real spiritual giant in their home. He graduated with honors from Delta High in May 1942, came to Cedar City to attend the Branch of Agriculture College (now Southern Utah University), but in July of 1943 he joined the Marines and spent the next three years caught up in the terror of World War II.

Back home in Delta at the war's end, Neil wasted no time in making the acquaintance of a beautiful brunette—"a

Springdale girl named Golda"—where she was working in her brother-in-law's cafe. Neither Golda nor Neil, even though having been reared LDS, were active Church members, and they were married in October 1946 in a civil marriage.

The newlyweds set up house in Delta. Two of their closest neighbors, Wayne and Beryl Sorenson, were the first of what would be many caring LDS friends who never gave up on the in-active couple. "I recall that it was over our back fence that Wayne once told me that if I would pay my tithing, I would never miss it," Neil says. But the faith to follow through was just not there.

Neil and Golda's family rapidly grew with the proud addition of four children. Douglas Neil was born in 1947, Marlys Renee in 1949, Harold Scott in 1950 and Linda Kay in 1957.

Just before Linda Kay's birth, Neil joined the Utah Highway Patrol. He was assigned to Grantsville in Tooele County, and continued there for the next decade. While serving in northern Utah, he was promoted to sergeant. But promotions and tenure notwithstanding, it seemed as though the family had a harder and harder time making ends meet; for years Neil worked a second job just to scrape by each month.

By 1971 the family had relocated to Cedar City, Utah, where Neil retired in '79 as a captain in the Highway Patrol. Yet, even with the children grown and gone, Neil and Golda were doing no better financially. Retirement was short lived as Neil once again entered the work force in an effort to make their income at least match the expenses. He and Golda often thought on the many times friends, neighbors and family had promised them over the years that if they would just pay a full and honest tithing, things would be better for them. But how could they even consider such a sacrifice when life circumstances always demanded more than they brought in? Now, they were challenged financially by Golda's increasing health problems.

"Over the years, especially as we were active with the Elk's, I had more than my share of cigarettes, coffee and social drinking," says Neil, "but we also always had good home teachers—especially after our move to Cedar City." With their encouragement Neil at long, long last, felt touched that he should try to live the Word of Wisdom.

In Neil's heart two desires were beginning to grow; to receive a Patriarchal blessing under the hands of his brother Vane (a Stake Patriarch) and to be sealed to his wife and parents in the St. George Temple. All of his brothers and sisters had undergone the ordinance work save for him. He fully understood that he had a ways to go to be worthy to enter the Temple. Between the Bishop's diligent home teachers, Neil's own change of heart, and most especially, the power of prayer, he successfully kept the Word of Wisdom. Neil says, "If I can do it, I know anybody can. The secret is to *invite the Lord in*. Golda and I felt we couldn't go just part way, but step-by-step we would meet our spiritual goals."

Neil's next big challenge was paying tithing. "I broke in cautiously by paying one third of a full tithe for two months, and when nothing calamitous happened financially, upped it to two thirds of a full tithe for another couple months. And, sure enough, everything was still going fine, so I went whole hog and started paying a full and honest tithe!"

The results? So many that the couple stands amazed, for they range from the small but appreciated to the incredible. Neil says,

"Lot's of things have happened since then that are true blessings in our lives, like . . .

"—we have come across items that have been long lost

"—the money just always somehow stretches to meet our needs every month. There's no more mad scrambling or working extra jobs to make do financially;

"—extra money comes in—like when our neighbors had linseed oil put on their shingles. The wind blew on our car and caused damage to the finish; after an estimate, an insurance company sent us a check. But after the work was done, it cost seventy-five dollars less than the estimate. The insurance company asked us to just keep the difference; said it wasn't worth the time in bookwork to change things;

"—and Golda's health; blood tests two years ago showed she had a cancerous tumor, but the doctors have never been able to find it! She still goes in every six months for more tests, but so far so good;

"—I am seventy-one years old now, and in spite of a battle with prostate cancer, my health is great."

Neil and Golda went to the St. George Temple on a sun-drenched spring day in May 1989 and were sealed to each other and to both sets of parents for time and all eternity. Serving as witnesses were the Bishop's neighbors of so long ago in Delta, the Sorenson's.

Neil was able to confirm to Wayne that his testimony of fifty years ago concerning the payment of tithes was absolutely true; "The thing that has been remarkable to us as tithe payers, is from struggling to get by with two jobs, our life is so enriched we have been able to not just save for ourselves, but to help other members of the family as needs have arisen.

"We know these changes came about from our desire to live God's commandments, clearing up things in our lives that were not right, putting ourselves in a position so that we could receive blessings, and the bottom line is, we really don't miss the income we turn in as tithing!" Neil concludes, "It has not been a burden at all."

"And Prove Me Now Herewith"
Billie and Bruce Sturtevant

He stands six feet, five inches tall, and people look up to soft-spoken, community, business and Church leader Bruce Sturtevant in more ways than one! He and his wife Billie have blessed the lives of many wherever they have lived over the course of their twenty-three-year marriage. As newlyweds they resolved to (1) commit themselves to faithfully adhere to the principles of the restored gospel, including the law of tithing, no matter how tough circumstances might be, and (2) never turn down an opportunity to serve the Lord. The results? Billie has served in every organization conceivable in leadership and teaching positions, and Bruce has served in numerous positions, including eight bishoprics—either as a counselor or as bishop.

Both Bruce and Billie were converts to the Church. Bruce was an Air Force brat, his family moving throughout the states over the course of his growing-up-years. He was the middle child, with an older brother and a younger sister.

His last two years in high school were spent in Hawaii, where his dad was then stationed. As a non-LDS high-school graduate, he chose to attend BYU-Hawaii for the incredibly non-profound reason that it was located closer to his favorite surfing beach than any other college! His older brother had chosen a career in the Air Force. He worked as a dental technician, assigned to a dentist who happened to be LDS. Back at home on leave, Robert challenged Bruce that if he would start taking the missionary lessons, Robert would join the Church. As it turned out, Bruce turned the tables by being baptized six months before his brother, during the summer of his sophomore year.

Bruce's dad at first was dead set against the boys joining the Church. But over the years, as he has seen the changes for the good in their lives, he now fully accepts their choice.

Shortly after Bruce's baptism in 1966, the family was transferred literally to the other side of the world to Washington, D.C. The family decided to take a cross-country road trip to arrive at their new post. They dropped Bruce off at BYU in Provo, Utah along the way.

Billie, on the other hand, was born and raised in the very same town, La Grande, Oregon. The youngest of three sisters, she pretty much grew up in the restaurant her parents owned and operated. Her family was not affiliated with any particular church. Billie attended her first year of college at Eastern Oregon State College, her second at the University of Oregon, and then, through the influence of LDS friends, she transferred to BYU. Within a year she was baptized—the same year that Bruce was, 1966.

Bruce was not at the Y long when he received a mission call to the Southwest Indian Mission (now the Arizona Holbrook Mission). After working for two years with the

Navajos, he returned to college. He and five other returned missionaries from the Lamanite mission cleverly managed to rent an apartment together; Bruce was called to be "father" of the BYU-organized student-family group that met once a week for family home evenings. There were twenty-six kids in their "family," a particularly close group out of which seven marriages were generated. In fact, Billie was one of those kids, and Bruce and Billie's union was one of the eternal marriages.

Bruce was only one semester away from his degree when the need for steady income became overwhelming. The newlyweds moved to Gallup, New Mexico for a job. A couple of years later they choose to follow up on what they hoped was the chance of a lifetime, the opportunity to own and operate a restaurant in Ellensburg, Washington.

Over the next five-and-a-half years the couple took on an astounding amount of responsibility. They often put in twenty-four-hour shifts at the restaurant. During these years they greeted five children into the family (Jennie in 1973, Tara in '75, Rebecca in '76, Matt in '80 and Andrea in '83). They also took in Billie's aged mother, who was blind. They cared for her until her death in 1983.

Even if Billie didn't have a work shift in the restaurant, each and every morning she delivered six freshly-made pies and home-made rolls to the restaurant. All of the soups and gravies served were also made from scratch. True, they were making ends meet, but family time together was just not there, and Bruce and Billie were getting "really tired of not having a family life," says Bruce.

They held a family conference, and decided that dad should return to college to complete a degree in accounting. This he did, taking advantage of Ellensburg's own Central

Washington State University. Through the course of the next three years, Bruce worked on his degree, worked two jobs to support the family, taught Seminary, and ultimately served their ward as bishop.

The day the degree was handed to him, the family figured the really hard times were behind them, but finding a job proved difficult and stressful, both for Bruce and for Billie, who had repeatedly applied for positions with the college.

They looked for weeks but no offers were forthcoming. Bruce explains, "As we continued to pay tithing, and obeying all other commandments to the best of our ability, our family felt that surely we had done everything we possibly could. Now, it was the Lord's turn; in family council, we decided, in essence, to put the Lord to the test. In family prayer that evening, we calmly presented to the Lord our case. We reminded Him of our obedience, ESPECIALLY to the law of tithing. We told Him we had done all we could, and now it was up to Him." Both Bruce and Billie felt confident that things would start clicking.

Within two weeks of their special family prayer, Bruce was offered a job with a "spanking new company," and that same week Billie was finally offered a position in personnel at the university.

On reflecting on their heavenly presentation, Bruce remembers how "we made a special point of reminding Father that we had been faithfully paying our tithing—no matter how bad the circumstances!"

Since that fateful week in 1984, Bruce has never been without employment, not for a single day, and as Billie has worked to augment family income, there has always been a job for her as well.

Paper Money

Lynnette Boyer

Lynnette Boyer had not done well in high school, and she had not done any "school-type stuff" in more than a decade since. She held the intimidating stack of application forms slightly away from her and stared aghast at the prospect of going to college. There was no choice. She was not trained for a career that would earn a living wage, and the doctor had made it very clear that her husband's days were numbered. Soon their family of six would be totally dependent on whatever she could earn.

With characteristic determination, Lynnette grabbed a pen and dove into the pile of forms. This ritual was performed in a timely way every year for the next three years. The mountain of paperwork yielded five grants and a subsidized loan to pay for her education. By March of 1987 all financing for her senior year at Whitman College seemed secure. Lynnette breathed a sigh of relief. A short-lived sigh.

June brought bad news. A review of her transcript revealed two more classes had to be squeezed into her senior year. This meant $300 more for books and fees. "I can handle this," Lynnette tried to reassure herself. But when the college announced a hike in tuition, the search for additional funding was on. Where could she find nearly $200 a month?

A mental review of options was depressing. Deadlines for grant applications were long past. No more loans were available. The children already had paper routes and the Boyers were living on a shoestring. Several creditors, especially the doctors and hospitals, were working with the family, making gracious concessions that helped tremendously. Each of her husband's surgeries cost tens of thousands of dollars. Not only were debts incurred with each operation, but income was lost during the increasingly longer recovery periods. Robbing Peter to pay Paul had become a monthly necessity. But, so far, she had not robbed the Lord.

So far. That unchiseled block of legal tender hung center stage in her mind. It would go a long way toward solving the problem. Maybe she could negotiate a delayed payment plan with the Lord. After all, it was working well for everyone else! Trying to talk herself into it nearly made her sick. But, with characteristic determination, she persevered, logically listing all the reasons why using the tithing money was a good idea. After carefully outlining a repayment schedule that stretched several years into the future, Lynnette was prepared to bargain with the Lord.

Armed to the teeth with logic and good intentions, she prayerfully petitioned for confirmation of her decision. She did not receive it, and she was not surprised. In fact, she was relieved. Paying her tithing felt wonderful that Sunday, even though it meant getting another part-time job.

Lynnette had resisted that option. Up until now she had worked while going to school, but the extended hours of absence from the home were taking their toll. Her family was crumbling under the pressure. Lynnette had to trust to the Lord to provide for all their needs, both financial and emotional. As she handed the tithing envelope to the bishop, all her hope and trust went with it. Handing in the tithing was hard, but giving control to the Lord was even harder! The very complicated situation was now completely in the Lord's hands.

That week, while scanning the want ads, a short notice caught her eye. The local newspaper was looking for a reporter; someone to cover school board meetings, city celebrations and local history. The job description screamed flexibility. It was a perfect solution! Eyes popping and heart racing, Lynnette proclaimed, "I can do that!" Her long-time residency in the area, her connections, and her knowledge of regional and personal histories gave her a competitive edge. One possible drawback: a sample of writing must be submitted with the application. The only one she had was a paper she'd written for school, but that would have to do!

Lynnette remembers, "One of the other applicants was a real journalist, with experience and everything!" But the editor, Rusty Bradshaw, wanted someone with connections. Exciting things were happening in little Athena, Oregon. Scandal was brewing in the ambulance service and the roof on the new school gymnasium had collapsed. He needed a reporter who knew the people involved. The "real" journalist was new to the area.

Lynnette was the best fit for the job and, of all her options, this job was the best fit for Lynnette. But it got better. When Rusty hired Lynnette, he broke with the paper's usual pay scale policy. Instead of paying her by the inch, he offered her a flat $200 per month. Flabbergasted, she gobbled out, "Yes! OK! That would be fine!"

Lynnette asserts, "The Lord really came through for me. Paying tithing works!"

When Less Means More

Adriana Perusia

It was Adriana Perusia's paternal grandfather who first came to Argentina from Italy. Fleeing the atrocities of World War I and eager to taste of the freedoms of the Americas, he travelled the Atlantic by himself, leaving family and friends behind, never to see them again.

The courageous young immigrant found work on a rural ranch near Santa Fe, Argentina, fell in love and married, and proceeded to welcome fourteen children into his family. The loneliness of starting out a new life on a continent half-way around the world from his birth home was soon forgotten. He worked his way up to the vital position of ranch foreman for the wealthy landowner.

His honesty was legendary, and it was childhood stories told at the knees of her father of her grandparent's integrity and kindness that made them angels-on-earth in Adriana's eyes: her grandfather worked long, hard days to ensure the ranch's annual profits. If one of the owner's cattle died, he would replace it with one of his own. If there was a crop failure, he would refuse payment for his services.

While the family proper had over a dozen children, Adriana remembers her father explaining that growing up on the ranch, they felt like there were a lot more than that! His family NEVER turned anyone away from lodging or meals. Since their house was always open to any passerby, his little mother never knew how many to expect for lunch or dinner.

"The family was not rich, but whatever they had, they would share with everybody," says Adriana.

"My father is every bit as honest as his parents were, and I think it was this honesty and humbleness that helped my parents to recognize the true Church when friends introduced them to it."

Adriana was sixteen when her parents started attending The Church of Jesus Christ of Latter-day Saints. Shortly thereafter, they were baptized. However, for Adriana and her older brother, their parents left it up to them. Adriana's feelings about needing membership in any church remained ambivalent until she turned eighteen. She really felt no need for religious involvement, but life events were progressing at a startling pace. She had married as a seventeen-year-old and was expecting her first child. One Sunday, having consented to come listen to her father give a talk in Sacrament Meeting, the Spirit finally touched her heart. "It was like listening to an angel," Adriana recalls, "and it started me on the road to baptism, but I still did not understand how Joseph Smith could be a prophet—that was my stumbling block to joining Christ's Church."

With the patient encouragement of her parents, Adriana finally consented to be baptized on May 15th 1976—the same day, she would later discover, that her one concern about the

Church—Joseph Smith, had been baptized. Her pregnancy to-date had been a difficult one, and the font water that freezing late-fall day (this was the southern hemisphere) was bitterly cold. Adriana hesitated before entering the waters where her beloved father stood waiting for her; she feared the water and was concerned for her baby's safety.

Seeing her trepidation, her father promised her, "If you have faith enough, nothing will happen to the baby." Trusting in her father and his absolute, unswerving honesty at all times in all things, Adriana stepped down into the water. As she walked towards her father, he held out his hand to her. In that moment of supreme love and trust, her body filled with a supernal calm.

After the baptism, even though she continued working sixteen hour days at the business in which she and her husband were partners, Adriana never had another moment's pain or worry about her pregnancy. Her first son, Marcos, was born in 1976, followed by daughters Anahi in 1978, Ayelen in 1984 and son Miqueas [Miky] in 1987.

As rapidly as the children came, the business far outstripped family growth. The many years of incredibly long days for Adriana and her husband were bearing remarkable fruit for the Perusias. By Miky's birth, they owned two large homes, one in Santa Fe for the work week, and one in the country for week-ends. Each home was beautifully decorated, filled with custom-made furniture and staffed by servants. Adriana's life was now that of an affluent young wife and mother in Argentina. The children were in excellent private schools. She was surrounded by family and friends, enjoyed satisfying work both within and outside the home, and life denied her nothing in the way of material possessions.

She and her husband began travelling as time permitted. At one point they made an extended visit to the United States, exploring many regions of the sprawling country. Her husband was immediately taken with the idea of relocating the family to the states. Adriana, however, found it a threatening idea. In Argentina, they had, literally, everything. Why did they need to even contemplate such a frightening move? Adriana spent many sessions at the Buenos Aires Temple presenting to the Lord her concerns, but the heavenly answer was always the same: "Go."

So the family sold everything: the two magnificent homes and the expensive furniture, in a one-day auction. "I remember vividly walking into my house the day of the auction. I was overwhelmed by the challenges we had committed to by the move. I sank down to my knees and started crying," says Adriana, "but the Spirit told me again, 'this is the right thing to do.' And I finally accepted it with every part of my being.

"I did not want a big scene at the airport on the day we left. I requested that my friends stay away. It was going to be hard enough to leave my dear parents, who did not know if they would ever see us again. Only my parents, an aunt, my brother and one friend—who would not stay away—came for the farewell. It was a horrible moment. I later learned that my father collapsed as the plane took off. My mother thought he had died from the shock of my leaving. But he was just overcome at our departure, and did recover.

"We left not just all of our family and friends, and all of our possessions, but over $1,000,000 in the bank from the sale of our material goods. That money was subsequently illegally appropriated by one of our former business partners, and we have never seen a penny of it."

The Perusias, now penniless strangers in a foreign land, rented a small home in a farming community in northeastern Oregon that sported a sizable population of Hispanic-speaking people. The Perusias barely spoke English, could not obtain employment, and without furniture slept on the bare floors of the tiny house.

The family took to picking up cans along the roadsides for income. Adriana finally secured a job as a maid for a demanding woman. She, who once directed her own contingent of household help, now scrubbed floors on her hands and knees.

One night, in family council, Adriana proposed that "Now, more than ever, we need the Lord's help. Let's give Him even more than He asks so that we may be blessed adequately for our needs." And the entire family agreed to pay eleven percent of any income—whether from pop can return deposits or from picking fruit or from housekeeping income—from any earnings the family saw the Lord would receive eleven percent.

The results of this heartfelt strategy were immediate and astounding. Adriana remembers walking into a local grocery store shortly after making this commitment to the Lord and running into Sister Edvalsen from the ward. Adriana had just enough money to buy milk, even though the family was in desperate need of so many food products, but most especially eggs. Sister Edvalsen spotted Adriana and pushed her cart over to her, announcing out of the clear blue, "I feel like buying eggs for you." And she did.

On another day another acquaintance's son, whom she had never met, brought bags full of groceries. His explanation as he dropped them by the Perusia's house: "I had the strongest impression while grocery shopping just now to get extra of everything and to drop them by your house. Do you mind?"

Did she mind? She was overwhelmed by the kindness of this stranger. It wouldn't be the last time that friends would bring food and presents by to the struggling family.

As they kept paying that extra one percent in tithing, both parents got steady jobs in the region serving as interpreters. Adriana says, "Frequently as I have translated, I feel like the words have been put into my mouth. I talk faster than I can think!"

Adriana graduated in the spring of 1995 with a 3.92 G.P.A. in Human Services and Social Work. While life in the United States has continued to present more challenges than she ever anticipated (she is now a single parent), she says that "The children and I still pay eleven percent on our income to our Lord. We will never stop. After Easter this year we had not a cent in the house. But I felt impressed to look into a certain bureau drawer. To my astonishment, it held four dollars. And this has happened more than once since then."

Her faith in the blessings of paying tithing is strong and sure. She says, "Heavenly Father will never leave us alone, never forget us because of our obedience to His laws. This I know for a surety. Blessings keep coming to us, even more than the challenges. If I pay the tithing, I know for sure that the Lord is bound. I learned this scripture a long time ago, and I know it works."

Adriana herself has now encountered life experiences that, along with those of her predecessors, will serve as character-building stories of personal courage and conviction for her own grandchildren.

In four words William Penn summarized the remarkable challenges and subsequent blessings awaiting for those who, like this Latter-day Saint, stay the course well: "No cross, no crown."

Always Enough

Mida and Phi Pedersen

The 1960's was a decade marked by unrelenting growth for the Pedersen family. By 1969, after a disastrous logging accident, a career change that meant completing a college degree and supporting a family at the same time, husband and father Phil Pedersen was at long last back to a half-way regular life schedule. He was working as an instrument technician for a mill. The Crown Zellerbach Pulp and Paper Mill was located on the Oregon side of the mighty Columbia River in the Pacific Northwest. Unlike his past days in logging, instead of arising at 4 o'clock a.m., Phil could now luxuriate in bed until 5:30 a.m.! As always, Mida made him breakfast and kissed him good-bye before he headed out the door for the picturesque ferry ride from Puget Island in Washington state to Westport, Oregon.

It was a real relief to the Pedersens to have the years of triple-duty for dad over. He'd carried a heavy load as a full-time college student, a full-time wage earner and, of course, husband/father/devoted church member. No, he didn't stop functioning in the latter capacities, but the college course work was all but behind them.

After completing his degree, the Pedersens moved their brood back to their Cathlamet home an hour west of Longview. It was comforting to be back amongst life-long friends and family. They picked up renovation work on the house that had literally been sliced into three pieces for the move from Longview along the narrow back roads of western Washington. It was now nestled on an acre of land close to the shores of the Elocohman River, surrounded by farmlands. The kids swam and fished along the silty banks of the river.

Mida kept a large garden, Phil had a wily old horse that would try to escape his grassy field for the neighbor's immaculately groomed yard whenever Phil wasn't home. With an insight that small children and large animals seem gifted with, the aging gelding knew just where to go and what to do to wreak the most havoc. He invariably headed to the only professionally kept grounds in the area, resulting in Mida's receiving a significant number of irate phone calls from the property owner. Phil finally decided that his own life might just be longer if the horse was boarded out elsewhere!

By the early seventies, Mida was more involved with parenting duties than she had ever imagined. Her own brood, now numbering five, swelled to seven children with the addition of two foster children. Word of the Pedersen's involved parenting style and home filled with love had spread through the community, and Mida found herself caring for nine-year-old Robby, who was mentally retarded, and twelve-year-old Julie, who was proving a handful for her own mother. Mida worked diligently with Robby on both homework and general life skills around the home. She had great success with him, and was gratified to watch his progress and pride grow commensurate with his new abilities. Julie, however, proved a real challenge in the two years she stayed with the Pedersens.

The children were not just more in numbers, but in size. David was eleven-years-old and already five feet eleven inches tall. The Cathlamet home had a generous ten-foot by twelve-foot kitchen surrounded with above- and below-counter cupboards. As soon as they walked into the house, David and his after-school buddy had an unvarying routine; they would look through every single cupboard for snack foods. Then, just for safe measure, they would look once more for anything that might have magically appeared while they were scarfing down their first finds. It was not unusual for David to eat a whole loaf of freshly baked bread in a single swoop through the kitchen! To meet the needs of exponentially growing stomachs along with a moderate grocery budget, Mida learned to "cook eggs in just about one million different ways!" Meat was just too expensive a protein source for the family of nine. So, she boiled eggs, poached them, and scrambled them; mixed them in a white sauce and served them over toasted home-made bread; made egg-salad sandwiches, egg salad, potato salad with eggs, and egg soufflés.

Many budget items were lessened or eliminated to meet the increased pressure on the food budget. Tithing, though, was an item that they would not live without. They could not give up the blessings they knew obedience to this commandment brought. It was always paid.

The honeymoon of just working a nine-to-five job was short lived with Phil's call to be branch president of the forty-active-member-strong Cathlamet, Washington branch. By 1972 that number doubled, due to the continuous and devoted efforts of active members in fellow shipping the less active. The little branch met in the local city hall. But, more often than not, branch members could be found at the Pedersen home. Mida recalls that besides her seven children, rarely did a day pass that she did not have a number of branch members' offspring in tow.

"It was nothing to come home from Church on Sunday," Mida says, "with our huge old Plymouth station wagon loaded with more than our own kids. I would scramble over bodies to get to the kitchen to get lunch served, and invariably receive a call from some parent just checking that possibly one, two, or three of her kids had hitched a ride with us. I would conduct a quick count of heads and discover that they had!"

The meal-time phenomenon of extra bodies evolved to also include two to five extra adults at dinner. Phil was still going to night school a couple nights a week, so if branch members wanted to catch him, their best chance was at dinnertime at the Pedersen's. "Of course," Mida graciously explains, "You can't eat in front of them, so we always invited them to eat with us."

And, so, the "miracle of the meatloaf," that is, "miracle of the egg casserole," also came about. The Pedersen's dining room table never had fewer than nine folk around it for the evening meal—including the bottomless pit that was David (he finally stopped growing at six feet five inches)—and most often eleven to fourteen people. Mida learned early on not to fret. "No, there were never left-overs to speak of," she remembers, "but, absolutely NO ONE ever left that table hungry. There was always enough of whatever I had fixed, including for unexpected guests, to fill everybody, no matter how many times they dished up."

In looking back over those incredibly lean financial years and the meals that they continually provided for dinner guests by the dozen, Mida recalls that their food storage was also the best it has ever been. "Even with all those children, and the costs associated with running our household, we had a wonderful one-year supply tucked away. Now it is just Phil and I. We don't owe a cent to anyone in the world—even our house is paid for—and I am ashamed of my food storage. I truly think there is a correlation between the actual amount of the sacrifice required and the subsequent blessings a person receives. The fact that we never skimped on paying tithing to the Lord during hard times and, in turn, no one ever left a meal hungry, is to me just the proof of the pudding."

A More Sure Formula
Gail and Ralph Lewis

It was a long life journey from Whittier, California to western Oregon for Gail Lewis, but the introduction of gospel principles along the road has enriched her trip immeasurably.

"I think that the very first time I heard about the Church I knew it was true," Gail Lewis recalls, "even though I was only a junior in high school—in Whittier, where I grew up—when I took the missionary lessons. Of course, it helped that my parents were very supportive, even though they never joined."

Gail was first introduced to the missionaries by her older sister who, on the advice of a high school counselor had attended Brigham Young University. Both young women were baptized, and after high school graduation Gail followed her sister to Utah to the Y.

Gail graduated from BYU with a degree in early childhood education. She taught kindergarten for three years, then returned to college for a special education certificate. She spent the next five years teaching elementary school in Lehi, Utah.

But it was to Stayton, the rural western Oregon community of her parents' retirement years, that Gail would time and again return along life's travels. Located in Oregon's Willamette Valley, the Stayton area is surrounded by bean and berry fields. It's a school kids' Mecca for summer jobs.

As a single adult, with college degrees and steady employment, paying tithing was an easy, unobtrusive practice for Gail. She had more than enough income to meet all of life's daily needs; writing out that monthly check for tithing was automatic and painless. Trust life to change that!

In 1986 Gail's father suddenly died, leaving her mother a widow. Gail returned to Stayton to live with her for the next year, helping her to settle financial matters and to come to terms with the loss of her husband. For Gail, this unexpected stay in the community would soon bear fruit of a much different kind than that found in its fertile fields.

She immediately became active in the local LDS ward. She especially enjoyed participating in the Single Adult group activities. Gail remembers one unforgettable Sunday when she took a moment, in between meetings, to peruse the foyer's bulletin board. "I was looking at a posting of upcoming Single Adult events when another single in our ward, Ralph Lewis, came up behind me and remarked 'Gee, if you want to go to one of those, I'd take you.'"

She did, and he did, and six months later they were sealed in the Seattle Temple for time and all eternity.

Ralph, who already had a college degree in industrial arts, returned to school and secured a special education degree. The couple were subsequently offered a teaching contract in the tiny school district of Jewel, Oregon.

Three years later, in 1991, Ralph accepted a job offer in the Milton-Freewater school district located in northeastern Oregon. Renowned as the fruit basket of the state, Milton's gently rolling hillsides grow everything from nectarines to specialty apples that are shipped as far away as Arabia and Japan.

By now they had three dynamite little boys. The family really looked forward to moving to a town where the nearest church and grocery store were closer than forty-five minutes away! What they weren't looking forward to was making the move on almost no money. After paying for the moving truck, first and last month's rent and security deposit on a house in the new-to-them community on the other side of the state, Gail and Ralph settled into their new home. Later that week they assembled around the kitchen table for the monthly ritual of paying bills.

Moving and housing expenses had reduced their savings to exactly $250. Tithing came to $200. The bills were already numerous; Gail says she took a look at the notes requesting money due, compared them to the amount of available cash, and calculated an inescapable negative net sum. She calmly announced to her husband, "We simply cannot afford to pay tithing. If we do, we will have only fifty dollars to last the entire month, and no bills will be paid." No advanced algebra classes were required to see that!

Ralph, however, saw a more sure formula in which the Lord was an absolutely immutable integer. He replied, "Because of this, we MUST pay tithing!"

The following Sunday they did, and, Gail recounts, "There I was with fifty dollars and a whole month ahead of us. I really didn't know how we were going to make it."

But that is when the miracles started. Having made the acquaintance of just a few of the local ward members, and not sure that she could even remember anyone's name, Gail was astounded when within the course of the following week she received numerous calls from families asking if she would provide day care for their children.

The Lewis' had certainly not shared their marginal circumstances with anyone, but the sum total of goods given to them rapidly multiplied.

One sister brought over two cases of canned goods. The couple in charge of a special young adult dinner dropped by a gargantuan supply of chili left over from the meal. Another new acquaintance brought by fresh vegetables from the cannery she worked at, including corn, peas and beans.

They made it through the month, never missing a meal nor being without money to meet their daily needs.

"As many times as we have gone through tough times, we still ask, 'OK, what are we going to do?',", says Gail; "Now we have five boys [Joel, Ted, Zachariah, Micah and Abraham] and making ends meet is forever a challenge. But we have learned to ALWAYS choose to pay tithing. It doesn't mean that tough times don't keep coming our way, but things always, always somehow work out; just like those sure-fire equations in Algebra 101."

"And I Will Rebuke the Devourer For Your Sakes"

Glenna and Michael Merket

The Book of Mormon records Christ's remarkable visit after His resurrection to his "other sheep," the people of the Americas. In his brief visit with the Nephites he shared many prophecies and instructed them in Gospel principles. He made a special point of quoting Malachi concerning payment of tithes and offerings, and specific blessings that are reserved for the faithful tithe payer:

> Bring ye all the tithes into the storehouse, that there may be meat in my house; and prove me now herewith, saith the Lord of Hosts, if I will not open you the windows of heaven, and pour you out a blessing that there shall not be room enough to receive it.
>
> And I will rebuke the devourer for your sakes, and he shall not destroy the fruits of your ground; neither shall your vine cast her fruit before the time in the fields, saith the Lord of Hosts. (3 Nephi 24:10-11)

Over the course of a nightmarish one-hour ride between hospitals in the late morning hours of a dreary December day in 1991, Glenna Merket realized the literal fulfillment of the Lord's promises in the Book of Mormon on behalf of her family. Prior to that day when her baby's well-being hung in the balance, Glenna had struggled with the concept of paying a tenth to the Lord, especially as she and her husband continued to face often insurmountable financial challenges. It was sometimes with bitterness that she considered the payment of tithes.

Glenna and Michael Merket are a couple whose sweet, gentle countenances and always-ready smiles belie the years of financial struggle they have faced since first meeting in Las Vegas, Nevada in 1982. There they were both employees at the Maxim Hotel. Michael was Mormon, Glenna was not—for long! He began courting the shy blonde on 23 September 1982, and they were wed a scant two and a half months later, on December fourth. Only one month later, Michael baptized Glenna a member of the Church.

Both Michael and Glenna were natives of the desert metropolis, and they chose to spend the next four years in that southern Nevada city. There their son Noel was born on 12 December 1983, followed by daughter Danielle who arrived on 25 June 1985.

December seems to be a month of memories for the Merkets, both in terms of happiness and danger. On 4 December 1984, Michael, Glenna and Noel were sealed as an eternal family unit in the Las Vegas Temple.

Small business is the backbone of American economy, and the challenge of the courageous entrepreneurs who put their time, talent and monies on the line for the pay back of career satisfaction and potential financial stability was a dream that pulled greatly at the Merket family. Michael and Glenna decided to give up their safe existence in Nevada to pursue the dream in northern Utah. In 1987 they bought a Miracle Ear franchise and moved their family to Orem, Utah. There they compressed a lifetime of learning into an action-packed time period; they entered self-employment with great hopes, but left it only twenty months later. Glenna remembers it as a "bittersweet time," but later commented that what happened then "seems so removed and unimportant now."

The couple retreated to regroup with family back in Las Vegas. There their last child, Vanessa Joy, was born 21 March 1990. Always goal-oriented and not afraid of hard work, the Merkets chose to enter the business world again, but this time somewhat on their own terms; they were now looking not just for steady income, but for a better quality of life than that proffered in the glitter and glitz of a world-renowned gambling town.

They moved to rural Cedar City, Utah on the western rim of the canyon lands of southern Utah. Michael initially worked with a hearing center, then once again opened up his own business. Of course, the always-present trade-off when a business starts up in a small community is a lot slower period for establishment of a clientele base, and inevitably, a lot smaller revenues. This was in spite of the fact that the region they were now living in was a Mecca for the retiree and the subsequent hearing loss often associated with that special population group.

But no matter the number of moves made over the first decade of their marriage, there were two constants in the Merket's lives: dedication to the Church of Jesus Christ, and marginal finances! The new venture in Cedar City proved no different. "From my baptism into the Church in 1983, I struggled with the commandment of tithing. Yet, as we paid our tithing things occasionally happened to relieve our burdens for a while and carry us through our day-to-day lives," Glenna remembers. Nevertheless, financial turmoil always seemed so much a part of daily life to her that, she says, "I sometimes felt a little bitter when paying tithing during those most difficult times." Where were those blessings that the Lord had so boldly promised in the scriptures?

With that mind set, Michael and Glenna faced the fact that their latest endeavor in the world of small business ownership was doing little better than the first. Glenna took a part-time job on graveyard shift at the Holiday Inn to make ends meet. It was during that discouraging period that, Glenna explains, "something happened that gave me an understanding of what a small sacrifice tithing had been."

Their youngest daughter, Vanessa, was twenty months old in December of '91, and usually was a ball of fire on the home front. But when Glenna got home from work, she found her toddler a very sick little girl. Listless and hot, her temperature steadily climbed. Glenna's concern escalated drastically when she tried to give the baby a drink and some medicine, only to discover a lesion the size of a nickel in the roof of her mouth.

Panicking, Glenna called Michael, who hurried home from work with their only car. They rushed Vanessa to the small, local clinic that provided the community's only emergency medical services. There two doctors and a nurse thoroughly examined the baby. The medical staff's concern was only too obvious to the frantic parents. Vanessa's fever was still climbing; she was by then dehydrated, her breathing fast and shallow, and she was only semi-conscious. The doctors had no explanation for the abscess in the roof of her mouth, nor could they offer any help but to send the family on down the freeway to a pediatric specialist in the larger town of St. George.

Before heading down the road, they picked up their two older children from school, and the father and an uncle hurriedly gave the baby a priesthood blessing. Glenna describes the one-hour ride south simply as "torturous." Their minds filled with ever more horrendous scenarios of what complications awaited Vanessa. As her condition further deteriorated, they pulled up to the hospital.

Inside the waiting room, Vanessa awoke and for the first time in hours was able to take liquids. As the family of five waited for the doctor to come into the examining room, the little patient began to perk up. Glenna could feel her fever had dropped sharply, and the tiny tot started talking and demanding to be put down.

A few minutes later, as Glenna lifted her up to the examining table, the Spirit spoke forcibly to her; "Look in her mouth" was the insistent message. Glenna obeyed immediately and, incredibly, found no sign of the abscess; there was no hole, no scar, not even any redness where there had only a short time earlier been a sizable and extremely angry pustule. So overcome was she by this revelation that she dropped to her knees next to the table. Knelt in thanksgiving, the relieved mother clearly heard the words, "The windows of heaven have opened and poured out a blessing greater than you can receive." She knew without a shadow of a doubt that her baby's miraculous cure was a direct consequence of their paying tithing.

Glenna explains, "There is no amount of money or material sacrifice that could ever compensate for the life of that child or the miracle that happened that day. I bear my testimony to you that Heavenly Father blesses us for our obedience in the things that are most difficult to each individual. He blesses us in ways we don't even recognize sometimes because they are spiritual and eternal blessings that can only be seen when looking beyond our temporal sacrifice."

"RETURN UNTO ME, AND I WILL RETURN UNTO YOU"

Terry and Pat Brame

Oh, sure. They had a lot of choices as to a chapel to attend for Church meetings. Indeed, there were three wards, all equi-distant from the little wheat town they were living in. Little, and (key word here) remote. All three LDS chapels were fifty long miles away. And if they failed to fill the car's gas tank on Saturday, then the twice-a-day pilgrimage was totally out of the question; ALL facilities in the central-Washington community closed their doors late Saturday afternoon. And then there was the treacherous winter weather on the plains of the arid region; the sky could be blue when they left home, and they could still encounter a raging blizzard half-way to Sunday meetings; driving snows that obliterated any sign of paved highway.

As much as Pat and Terry Brame loved living in the rural community of Odessa, Washington, its very isolation proved a detriment to spiritual growth. It was a slow and unsuspecting slide that they took away from living gospel principles. Church attendance was predicated on so many things: surviving small, bored children on the long drive, cooperative weather, a full gas tank—all of these variables stacked the deck against regular attendance. Along with a growing laxness in attendance crept in a similar attitude towards paying tithing. If the bills were a little too overwhelming, it was simply skipped.

Unfortunately, weak fellowshipping by ward members did not help matters any. In the many years in the farming community, Terry saw her visiting teacher only once. The family never saw a home teacher. Only once were they invited to dinner by a ward family so that they did not have to make the time-consuming, gas-eating trip twice on Sunday. This was in the '70's and the Church was still on a split-meeting schedule.

So the Brames found themselves making the easy—rather than the right—decisions when it came to living gospel-related principles and practices. Not that they had ever had anything but a good example of gospel living; both were raised in active LDS families in western Washington. In fact, they had met at a stake dance in high school. They were married in June 1970, the week after Pat completed his freshman year at college. Terry had graduated the day before with a nursing degree from Lower Columbia College in Longview, Washington. Talk about a stress-filled, memorable week!

Three years later Pat completed a bachelor's degree from Whitworth College in Spokane. His major was in elementary education, his minor in art, and the young couple were none too picky about accepting an offer—any offer—for that first just-out-of-college job. It soon came, from a rural school district representing, among other small wheat farming communities, Odessa, Washington. Incredibly, the school board was looking for a sixth-grade teacher who also could teach high school art and coach football; it was a job tailor-made for Pat's abilities and interests.

And so they found themselves in Odessa, seventy miles from Spokane. The years there passed quickly and fairly uneventfully. The gradual slide in dedication to living gospel principles was something that only dawned on them after the fact. It was with a general sense of uneasiness as the decade of the '70's came to a close that the couple took stock of their spiritual, as well as their temporal growth as a family.

By 1980 Pat and Terry had four children, Wendy (now a BYU graduate and returned missionary), Brian (currently a college student in Portland, Oregon), Brandi (now a high school junior) and Beth (now a highly active seventh grader). And Pat was ready for a job change.

He accepted an offer with the St. Helens School District in northwestern Oregon as a teacher at St. Helens Junior High. They moved from the high, dry, sunny climate of eastern Washington to the rain-satiated overcast skies of the west coast. It was more than a geographical return to their old stomping grounds; the family made a commitment to returning to a gospel-centered life. Terry and Pat realized that while they had grown up under the loving tutelage of parents committed to living gospel principles, they, as a couple, had never consciously made that same commitment. While preparing for the move, they did so. Important to that commitment was rededication to attending Church regularly and consistently paying tithes, regardless of the particular financial situation on any given week.

Pat began work at the junior high teaching academics, again employing his sports-related skills as a wrestling coach. One afternoon, while showing a student a particular wrestling move, Pat wrenched his knee. It was a fluke thing, nothing that could have been anticipated or avoided. Nevertheless, the injury meant medical treatment and a recuperation period.

The Brame's medical bills were covered under the terms of their school-district-supplied health insurance, and it was a tremendous relief to the family to have the sizable bills relative to the knee injury covered. As far as they knew, once the treatments ended, everything was taken care of. They had duly turned in all forms, and they were sure that one day Pat would again walk just fine and would be able to continue teaching, coaching, and living a perfectly normal life.

Life was once again on a fairly even keel; Terry was working part-time at the Columbia District Hospital as a nurse, and Pat was back on the job with the junior high. That is, until Terry found herself expecting child number five!

She continued working as long as she could, the $500-a-month income from her job a vital part of the formula for making monetary ends meet. As the due date approached, Pat and Terry held a parents' summit on just how they would make do financially during her three-month leave of absence at the baby's birth. Terry recalls, "We dithered about sliding into old habits and postponing paying tithing until I was back on the job." But, after a prayer together, Pat felt strongly that they should trust that "somehow the Lord will provide." That was on a Sunday morning. That same day they turned in a full tithe.

Two days later, sixteen long months after Pat's knee injury, a check arrived in the mail from the State. It was a check made out for the exact amount the three-month leave would deprive the family of—$1,500, offered as a settlement for the disability resulting from the accident. The Brame's were astounded! Almost a year and a half after the incident? They thought everything had long ago been taken care of with payment of the sizable medical bills.

Daughter, Chanie, made her appearance in the family shortly thereafter.

Pat says, "We are now firm believers in tithing. So many little things have happened over the years, over and over again, to confirm the importance of obedience and subsequent blessings received."

If, Then

Lorelle Kirby Loosle

Lorelle Kirby Loosle was in fifth grade when the Holy Spirit first touched her heart. If she was to pinpoint a moment when her testimony began to grow, separate from that of her parents', it was an early winter morning as she flew around the house, desperately searching for the newest book in the "great book" series her school had embraced. It was Thursday, and every Thursday—on threat of death (at least in the mind of a sensitive fifth grader)—the books were due back at school. And Lorelle could not find her book anywhere.

She searched under beds, behind the sofa, on counter tops and in her sisters' rooms, but the little volume was just no where to be found. As the time to catch the bus approached, Lorelle was beside herself with worry. Finally, she decided to take her parents and Church teachers up on their oft-repeated entreaties to go to Father in prayer when in need. Hurriedly she knelt beside her bed and sincerely asked

Heavenly Father for help. As she waited for an answer, the ticking of the hall clock became the focus of her hearing. As the big old clock went tick, tock, tick, tock, she distinctly heard the message in sync: "look, up, look, up." So, she did; there on the top board of her bedroom shelving was the book.

"At that moment," Lorelle says, "I knew there was really something to what everyone had been telling me." The seed had been planted, but a personal testimony of each and every doctrine of the Church of Jesus Christ would be something that would come gradually over the years.

It was easy in her growing-up years to simply rely on the solid testimony of her family. Lorelle grew up in Salt Lake City, the daughter of parents who could trace their genealogies back to early Church converts. Her mother's great grandparents joined the Church in their native Denmark and immediately left the old world for Zion. Her father's family came from England. She was veritably surrounded by relatives, for by the time she made her appearance on earth, several generations of descendants were all still Utahns.

The family, regardless of size, has remained close, and Lorelle grew up with annual family reunions a way of life. "They have gotten a little crazy as time goes on," she says. She still especially cherishes the memory of traditional family auctions held to raise funds for future reunions—auctions always emceed by her grandfather, an auctioneer who takes into account the financial situation of each bidder. As the years pass he has become more didactic in his role, and may ante up the price of a beautiful home-made quilt to beyond its value, and then a moment later award crocheted clothing or hand puppets for a bid of a dollar or two to the first young, financially struggling bidder to open her mouth!

Even without her sizable extended family, life at home was a rich gospel-oriented experience. Lorelle was the oldest of five girls, and the daughter of a family which hosted thirteen foster children and exchange students. Their second foster son, a five-year-old named Johnny, had a particular impact on Lorelle's life. The young boy was deaf, and under the influence of Johnny and a good friend of Lorelle's who was also deaf, she developed an active interest in learning sign language.

The Kirby clan held family home evening regularly, and Lorelle vaguely recalls lessons on the law of tithing at one time or another. But it was really her parents' consistent example of paying tithing that impressed Lorelle. As a teen she regularly paid tithing on any baby-sitting earnings, not because she knew it was the right thing to do nor that she truly believed she would get blessings for doing so, but because she was sure her parents would be disappointed if she did not. It was out of a sense of duty and no more.

Lorelle decided to attend Utah State University in Logan, Utah in 1989, majoring in elementary education and minoring in deaf education. She put herself through college, relying on a four-year scholarship for tuition and fees. For board, room and books she relied on a series of jobs—everything from holiday baby-sitting to customer service at Albertson's.

It was while in college that she discovered that Church could be fun! She first went to meetings because there would be people there that she really wanted to see. Then she realized that the class lessons were actually applicable, and then she "just decided I liked the whole experience," not just because she knew she should be there, but because she wanted to be there.

During those touch-and-go financial years in college, a corollary slowly dawned on Lorelle. If she either forgot, or could not justify paying tithing (other needs were, after all, so very pressing), then she would invariably not get the job she was applying for. If, however, she turned in to the Lord His tenth, work always, always materialized. At the beginning of her sophomore year she recognized the pattern. The results were unvarying! Astounded at the reality of the Lord's promise to "open the windows of heaven" in return for obedience to the law of tithing, Lorelle committed to be a one hundred percent tithe payer at all times.

That year she fell into a housing job as a dorm activities rep, which was, as she describes it, "Having fun and getting paid for it!" By her junior year the job provided her with free housing for the balance of her college education.

Lorelle never again had to scramble for funding, nor was she desperate for a job. She now had a firm testimony of the corollary—if you consistently and honestly pay tithing, then the Lord must bless you as you stand in need.

Lorelle is now a part-time fifth grade teacher and with her husband Steve, parent of a fourteen-month-old daughter, Miriah. "Mostly," she says, "I will teach Miriah by example the importance of the law of tithing. But, being a teacher, I also really want to share the tithing principle with her by formal lesson in family home evening; I want her to know why she should be obedient to this law—not just because I say so, but because there is good *reason* for it."

Good Things Happen
James Connor Backus

James Connor Backus needed money. He wanted to go skiing when the snow came, and snow came pretty early in Pagosa Springs, Colorado. A second goal of equal importance concerned his savings account. A feeling of satisfaction filled him when he thought of how nice it would look when his savings book read $500. The youngest of six boys, Connor knew without asking that no one was going to give him the money he wanted, no matter how cute he was. He needed a job!

Ten-year-olds have a hard time finding work on their own, so Connor enlisted the aid of his older brother Cody. At thirteen, Cody already had a reputation as a hard worker. They looked for a job that they could share.

Fortunately, 1994 was a good year for apples and somebody had to sell them. The boys knew that they could do it. Abe agreed. And Abe owned an orchard. They struck a bargain: Abe's apples against Cody's and Connor's labor. At the end of the season, the boys would give fifty percent of whatever they made to Abe and split the rest between them. Connor was delighted, but Cody quickly became disenchanted with the idea. The truth was that Cody did not enjoy sales. He preferred other kinds of work; almost any other kind of work.

An impish grin danced across Connor's face as he listened to his brother talk himself out of the job. That was just fine with Connor. Fewer salesmen meant more commissions in his pocket!

His compact little frame seemed even smaller as he stood in front of the thirty bushel boxes, but he was not intimidated. Connor had been blessed with more energy than five ordinary people shared. He could handle this job alone. Excitement raced from his bright, blue eyes.

Telephones rang all over town as the newest fruit vendor made initial contact. These healthy, tasty, economical snacks were offered to friends, Church members, neighbors and acquaintances. He even tried to place samples of his product in the teacher's lounge at school in an effort to broaden his market, but was regretfully refused. There were rules against that sort of thing. In his most professional manner, Connor answered each customer's questions with a prompt and cheerful "Yes, sir!" or "No, ma'am!" In return for his courtesy he got smiles, praise, and orders.

Connor painstakingly recorded every customer's name, the date, and the quantity purchased, then carefully figured out how much was profit. He wanted an accurate account so he could pay Abe every penny he deserved. All the money was immediately deposited in the age-old bank—a tin can.

As the weeks passed, the air turned crisp while the apples turned soft. It was time to mail Abe his money. A final tally in the record book revealed profit for the season: $156. The money in the can matched the tally in the books. Simple math divided Abe's share from his. With another simple computation, Connor divided his share from the Lord's.

Shaking his head, he stared at the little stack of money in front of him. A moment ago there had been a big pile of it! Mixed emotions ran through him; pride at keeping such accurate records and depression at what the records revealed. Irrefutable evidence now lay before him: he could not meet his goals. Oh, sure, the passbook would plump up, but not quite to the magic number. And there would be no skiing. A miserable ten-year-old turned pleadingly to his mother. Tender sympathy laced a brief "good things happen when you do what's right" pep-talk.

Deciding to dispose of the money quickly before temptation could set in, Connor immediately stuffed the Lord's share into an envelope for the Bishop and readied his own share for deposit. That left Abe's share. Suddenly, Connor realized that he did not know where to send it! Up until now their contact had been through the telephone or in person.

What was Abe's address? Connor made his final business call. Abe was delighted to hear of their success, but did not give Connor his address. "You keep it," Abe told him. Astounded, Connor thanked him. And thanked him. And thanked him. Connor's joyful chatter burst through the house like Fourth of July fireworks. He was convinced: good things happen when you pay your tithing!

A Burning Testimony

Charity and Scott Shakespeare

The Bel-Franklin apartments in Spokane, Washington could best be characterized as a terrific source for "back when" stories. Up five flights of stairs was one particular apartment with a nozzle-less tub and a kitchen whose counter was "due in any day now." Calling it "home" was a culture shock for the newlyweds, but home it was. Their new situation had caused Scott and Charity Shakespeare to rethink many things they had always taken for granted, like the beautiful homes they had grown up in, and like food, clothing, familiar faces and loving family. Scott lay in bed one Sunday morning early in December of 1992, thinking about those changes and wrestling with the most pressing one . . .

Money. Tithing. Bills. Bills. Tithing. Money. Bills had deadlines with immediate consequences. As nice as it was to pay tithing from every check, it didn't seem practical this time. They could catch up next week and no one would be the wiser. It seemed a perfect solution from every angle except one: Charity. When he'd suggested that this brief delay might be the solution they needed, her response had been unequivocal. "What do you mean—'not pay tithing'? There's no question. We'll pay tithing!" He was unprepared for the strength of her response. It was like asking her not to breathe for a week!

In the few, short weeks they had been married, Scott had discovered that hidden within Charity's incredible sweetness were a few pieces of flint. Strike them and sparks flew. These were areas of no compromise. He knew he'd hit one with his tithing suggestion. He definitely believed in the principle of tithing, but working it in around the bills was a skill he did not have yet and really didn't see why he couldn't take some time to acquire it.

The money from their pay checks was in an envelope on the bookcase behind the front door. Virtually all the money they had was in that envelope. It was enough to take care of the week very nicely. Then he looked at his wife's face on the pillow next to his. "But," he thought, "life is longer than one week." He knew the right thing to do was to pay his tithing, and with this thought, the internal tug-of-war came to an end.

Scott had to work that afternoon but Charity was able to go to Church. Anticipation tingled through her as she got ready. Maybe she would have a chance to really get acquainted with someone today. It was getting pretty lonely.

While preparing for Church, work, and selecting what homework assignments he could possibly make headway on during slack times, Scott didn't notice Charity take ten percent of the money out of the envelope on the bookcase. As they knelt in morning prayer, Charity didn't realize the early morning struggle her husband had been through. Protection for their apartment, their belongings, their car and their persons was always high on their list of requests, and this morning's prayer was typical. The requests were constant, the words unchanging, the sincerity deep. Neither of them realized that the tithing that Charity would pass to the Bishop that day would bind the Lord to answer their prayer.

The day passed as planned, except that Charity again made no new friends . . . maybe next Sunday. Charity spent a solitary evening in the apartment. She was really looking forward to picking Scott up and hearing about his day. Snow was falling from a blackened sky as she locked the door to their apartment. Scott's shift ended at eleven o'clock that Sunday night, and she wanted to be there on time.

Driving down Division Street on their way home, the couple noticed flashing lights and confusion around their apartment building. Shaking their heads and cracking jokes about what they had a feeling might be the third false fire alarm in as many weeks, they circled around to the alley behind their apartment.

The alley was blocked; they had to park next door at the Goodyear Tire Store. Unlike the other times, everything was very quiet. Maybe this wasn't just a false alarm. Walking around to the front of the building was like entering a kaleidoscopic world of spiraling snow and pulsating emergency lights accented by the terse, staccato tones of rescue workers. Neighbors with sooty faces stood in the tarnished snow, their silence contributing to the din swirling around them.

Looking up, Scott and Charity could see nothing but broken, charred windows advancing from the main door to the end of the building. The fire had been contained on their floor. The building manager saw them and answered the unspoken question in their eyes with a negative shake of his head.

They watched the fire fighters with growing concern. All that they possessed was surrounded by fire. Penetrating cold finally drove them to the warmth of a Greyhound bus that had been hired to house the displaced tenants. The air inside the bus was saturated with the muted weeping of the worn, the exhausted, the conquered. But Scott refused to be conquered. Taking his wife by the hand he announced, "We're not staying here."

"Oh, good," she thought, "he knows what to do."

That wasn't exactly true. He just had to get out of there. Walking through the commotion, they cut through the alley and headed toward their car. Gazing at the little black hole of their apartment's window brought the silent recognition that everything they owned was probably in ashes.

Charity's reactions bordered on hysteria. Scott remembers her crying out, "I left a light on! It's not on now! Everything's gone! Where are we going to go? What are we going to do? We don't know anybody in this town!"

"For some crazy reason," says Scott, "I really believed that explaining why they turn the power off during a fire and pointing out that no one had lights on would make a difference in Charity's emotional state." Fortunately, he was a quick learner. Cutting his logic short, he took her firmly by the hand and began walking them quickly towards their car. Charity needed to see some action—any kind of action. This was the first time Scott's little family had truly faced a crisis. He had to figure out what to do. They needed help, but from where?

Between their work and school schedules, they were only shadows on the Church walls. Yes, they had met people, but they didn't really know anyone. No name, no friendly face came to mind. They had no credit cards. All their money was on the bookshelf in their apartment—if they still had an apartment.

Then Scott remembered that his mission president, Larry Call, was still in Spokane. Hope surged as he pulled over to a roadside phone booth and dialed President Call's home. No answer. Scott was desolated, but there was no other option. Their little car could barely climb the icy hills as they headed for President Call's home. Shock was finally setting in. They had to get off the streets soon.

A sleepy, bewildered man in a bathrobe opened the door in response to Scott's persistent knocking. Charity watched as an expression of concern and compassion swept this good man's face. The door swung wide. A haven was offered. Soup and sympathy calmed her jangled nerves, and exhaustion brought numbed sleep. Charity had reached her limit. Everything would have to wait until tomorrow.

But Scott couldn't sleep. His term project—a bust portrait of William Shatner (Captain Kirk of TV's "Star Trek") was due in the morning. It had taken fifteen hours to complete. A wave of nausea swept through him as he remembered how he had laid it on the coffee table that very morning. He did not take it to work because he was afraid it might get smudged. As the irony of the situation struck him, he marveled at how a person could laugh and feel sick to his stomach at the same time. Now Captain Kirk of the Starship Enterprise had faced the final frontier alone.

Scott was well aware that success in college equated to financial success for his newly founded family. The burden of doing well in his course work was heavy. All his notes, his books, his projects had been in the apartment. Facing finals week without them was overwhelming. The night was interminable.

Morning found Scott slowly climbing the apartment building stairs to take stock of their losses. As he turned the corner to begin the fourth flight of stairs, it started getting dark. It was hand-in-front-of-your-face black on the fifth flight. He couldn't see the floor to check for weak spots. It smelled of wet, charred wood. Scott retreated to the manager's office to borrow a flash light.

Guided by the dingy light emitted from two worn batteries, Scott stepped carefully along smudged walls. He stood transfixed at the landing on his floor. The melted carpet held splinters of glass that had fallen as the firefighters had worked their way down the hall. Even the elevator was seared and melted!

A sharp S-turn in the hall would bring him to their apartment door. With heart pounding, Scott took a few more steps. The walls went from brown to decimated! The wavering smudge from the flash light only served to make the destruction more overpowering.

As he turned the last corner, Scott saw a bright light. It was coming through the door to their apartment. The thinner panels in the door had been burned out. The door itself was slightly ajar and hanging at an angle. Surrounded by the charcoal walls, Scott braced himself and pushed open the door.

Bright sunlight flooded the room. A light dusting of ash covered the familiar furnishings. Furnishings? Yes! Furnishings! Their apartment looked just as they had left it! Scott was more stunned by the survival of their belongings than he had been by the devastation in the hall. He rushed to the coffee table. Someone had placed a piece of posterboard over his portrait of William Shatner. Captain Kirk was unharmed! He silently blessed the unknown firefighter.

Waves of happiness and gratitude turned to complete awe as Scott realized the magnitude of their protection. The door had burned through. The carpet was melted in a foot-wide arc around the door, stopping directly in front of the small, cheap bookcase that held all the money they had in the world. The telephone, the CD's in their plastic cases, and the stack of paper on the shelf were all in perfect condition. There was just a little soot on them. The other side of that wall was totally blackened.

Every other occupied apartment on their end of the building was gutted. Nothing salvageable. No shading. No variation. All black. Yet they could see where a bubble of protection started around the door with the melted floor and smoke-damaged ceiling in a twelve-inch arc. Scott and Charity realized that they had been protected by a force other than nature, and they realized that this was a fulfillment of the Lord's promise, "Bring ye all the tithes into the storehouse . . . And I will rebuke the devourer for your sakes." (3 Nephi 24:10-11.) Since then tithing has never been an issue between them. They have a burning testimony of it.

A Strong Witness

Sandra and Mick Strong

Twenty-one years piloting a helicopter for the Coast Guard's Search and Rescue Division was the closest thing to heaven a job could ever offer: flying, yet coming home every night. Now they wanted to ground him. The next promotion would land him a desk job in Washington, DC and obligate him for six more years of service. Should he stay in or retire?

Mentally balancing the tempting security of the service against the not-so-tempting idea of raising his children in the nation's capital was a painful, yet brief, exercise. Paul was fifteen, Stacey, twelve; the triplets—Adam, Aaron and Heidi—were only six, and Elizabeth brought up the rear at an energetic age four. Being landlocked in a metropolis was definitely not in the future for this crew.

With a deep breath, crossed fingers and mighty prayer Mick and Sandra Strong said good-bye to military paychecks that came like clockwork, terrific medical benefits, and the warmth of Pensacola, Florida. For the next three years Sandra kept the home fires burning while Mick devoted himself to earning a bachelor's degree in dental hygiene. When times were tough, it helped to know that a friend was holding a job for Mick in Port Angeles, Washington.

And times were tough. Retirement income was only one-fourth the amount of active duty pay. It would take a miracle to meet the family's growing needs. Mick remembers prioritizing their meager income. "No matter how high the water got, tithing got paid!" Then, miraculously, each time a need arose, a way to meet it followed.

As a musical family grows, a piano becomes a must. Sandra was puzzling over how she could get access to one when the phone rang. A distraught neighbor pleaded for help; her husband would not understand this time. Could Sandra help her out? The confirmed yard sale junkie confessed to buying a piano that very morning. It was in perfect condition and only fifty dollars! The people just wanted to get it out of their basement. Only after she got home did she stop to think; she already had a piano! What was she going to do with TWO pianos?

A huge grin crept across Sandra's face as she remembered the note from Mick's mom that had arrived that very day. "Don't know why I'm sending this," it read. "Hope you can use it!" "It" was a check for fifty dollars! Sandra was delighted to help her neighbor out!

For those three years the family was shortchanged because of academic demands. Now graduation and employment were a month and a state exam away. Half-packed boxes and cleaned out closets marked the countdown to Port Angeles and a normal family life. Then, one evening in May, the bell on the telephone shattered all the plans and dreams.

Unhappy events caused their dear friend to sell his business and move away from Port Angeles. Now, after all their effort and sacrifice, there was no job waiting. Disappointment and despair were replaced with peace and a sense of purpose when the Strongs knelt in prayer. An impression to go job-hunting in Port Angeles filled both of them, so they made preparations immediately.

Their visit coincided with the dedication of the Port Angeles chapel, a delightful surprise. All the former bishops were asked to speak at the dedication and Mick accepted with great pleasure. Joy in the growth and success of the ward helped to balance the growing depression of the unsuccessful search for employment.

Sunday, as Mick took his place on the stand, he visited briefly with the stake presidency. Mormon introductory conversations tend to get directly to the heart of the matter. Are you here permanently or just visiting? Do you play the piano? What do you do for a living? (Translation: Are you available week nights?) In no time Mick's strengths and concerns were discovered. Grins chased through their little circle as the solution to Mick's problem stepped forward in the form of the first counselor, Frank Pitcher. President Pitcher was a dentist from the other end of the stake and he needed a hygienist. Had the Strongs come job-hunting any other time, they would not have met him.

Only the state exam remained between the Strongs and an adequate income. Mick was an excellent student and had chosen his new profession well so the family was not worried. They bought a house in Silverdale and settled in.

Cheers went up as the scores for each part of the exam came in. Oral prophylaxis (cleaning), carving (sculpting a filling to a perfect fit), written and local anesthesia—all very difficult—were passed with flying colors. They were stunned when Mick failed the easy one—patient evaluation! The next state exam was nine long months away.

The Strongs prayerfully made two decisions: to double their fast offering and round their tithing to the nearest whole dollar. The Spirit whispered that, if they did this faithfully, all would be well with them. However, a whopping $293 power bill didn't fit the "all would be well" impression. Where would the money come from? Consciously asserting their faith, the Strongs clung to the Lord's promise. He did not fail them. Fulfillment came in a sweet letter from an honorable friend who was finally able to repay the $300 the Strongs had loaned and forgotten long ago.

The thrill of facing potential disaster ebbed and flowed continuously. Taking stock of their resources, Mick always asked himself the same question, "Would you rather have ten-tenths to spend or nine-tenths and the Lord? I think the latter is the better resource."

The Strongs kept their commitment of offerings. During those months, short-term work opportunities came when cash needs were most pressing; family unity grew as Mick began to fully participate in his children's lives once again; Sandra's honey-do list became a priority and Mick installed a shower, built shelves and repaired the deck. The harmony of a house in order was a very sweet blessing. A holiday-season job even provided Christmas presents for all the children.

Mick still marvels as he recalls, "The Lord kept our family afloat with blessings of all shapes and sizes—too many to count or to be able to tell about. After I passed the exam and went to work, the extra blessings no longer came, but I know if I ever need them, I will have them again. Obedience to the law of tithes and offerings brings a wealth of spiritual and temporal blessings. I am a witness."

Attitude, Gratitude and Heavenly Blessings

Years later, and it is another Relief Society lesson, this time centering on gratitude. The sister teaching the lesson draws on the experiences of a Dutch family who endured the horrors of World War II. The ten Booms lived in Amsterdam. A Christian family in more than name only, they sheltered dozens of Jewish citizens who were fleeing the Holocaust at great risk of their own lives. Mama and then Father died, but the sisters, Corrie and Betsie, continued their humanitarian efforts until their work was discovered and they were placed in a concentration camp.

Soft-hearted, spiritually-minded Betsie, even in the nightmare world of a concentration camp with death and disease and forced labor and starvation their daily fare, could always find something for which to feel gratitude. But the night she started thanking the heavens in prayer for the fleas that infested their barracks, Corrie really thought she has gone over the edge. Years later, Corrie discovered the reason the women of their barracks, and their barracks alone, had gone unmolested by the guards was the fleas. An attitude of gratitude on the part of one faith-filled woman had ensured the continued blessing of protection the minuscule pests afforded the prisoners, in spite of their ignorance of heaven's hand in their plight.

Anita remembers a time when, left a single parent with marginal income, she desperately wanted to provide her children with a home. Not a rental, not an apartment above a garage, nor a damp basement lodging, but a real *home* where they could plant a garden and fence in a yard for the pets, and really set down roots. For six long months she looked, eventually finding a three-bedroom Veteran's Administration repo that had sat empty for over two years. The roof leaked like a sieve and had caused extensive damage to the interior ceilings and walls in several rooms. But from the first moment she stepped onto the porch and peaked through the slit of a window on the front door, she just knew it was the home for her little family. And even with a new roof in the offing and interior repairs, (it was to be sold strictly *as is*) the price was a bargain for 1987—only $21,500. But, the Spirit restrained her from entering into contract for the house.

She remembers telling the heavens in no uncertain terms what she thought of this state of affairs. "I felt, for all the world, like a four-year-old whose mom has just told her to not play at her friend's house and to come directly home. Since it was a cold, rainy January when I saw that little house, I could just see myself in a yellow raincoat and rubber boots, a thunderous scowl on my face, sloshing through every deep, wet, muddy puddle I could find on the way home. In my mind, I told Heavenly Father off for such a sick joke; showing me the home I knew was right for my family, and then not letting me buy it. I humphed long and loud, but in the end the answer was still NO. No explanation, just 'No, not now.'"

We remained in our miserable little rental, paying tithing and keeping all other commandments to the best of my ability.

Three months later I was contacted by the realtor representing the property. The V.A. had lowered the price to an unbelievable $18,500 and had, incredibly, replaced the entire roof. And it was still sitting without a buyer. He explained, however, that the buyer would still have to fix the interior water damage at his own expense.

This time, the Spirit shouted "Go for it!" And I did!

Now I could see the wisdom in the Lord not letting me make the purchase earlier that winter. We had managed to save just enough for the down payment. There was no way I could ever have afforded to fix the roof. And, now, it was completely taken care of.

And then something else happened that let me know that Heavenly Father really is concerned with us and involved in our lives more than we know, just waiting for us to allow Him, through our obedience, to work wonders. While the house sale was in closing, I made a habit of dropping by whenever I was in the neighborhood. If I was headed across town to a meeting in the morning (I was working as director of a chamber of commerce at the time) I would swing by to take a look at the house. Or, at lunch I would grab a sandwich and eat it on the back porch at the house. Often, after work I would pick the children up at our rental and we would take a quick tour of the little soon-to-be-our-very-own home. Not once did we see a worker (to this day I wonder about that), but for weeks the interior of the house was littered with the tools and materials needed for repair of the sagging, ragged ceilings and mildewed walls.

I talked with the realtor about this, and asked him how it was that the V.A. was going ahead with repairs to the interior. He assured me that whatever I was seeing was most certainly not the V.A. at work; the house was AS IS, and AS IS was how the contract was being closed by the seller.

At one point I even invited him to go by and see the work-in-progress going on inside the house. He refused point-blank, telling me that after thirty years representing V.A. repo's, he knew what he was talking about, and there were no repairs being undertaken by the V.A. at my little house.

I never brought the subject up again, but on 1 May 1987 when we moved into that funny little house, the ceilings throughout looked brand new, and the walls were without blemish.

I still break into a cold sweat when I think of my short-sighted attitude, and the lack of gratitude I exhibited for the Lord's guiding hand in my life.

It is so easy to curse the heavens when life seems particularly harsh and unfair. But through the accounts shared in this volume, we see a pattern of certain attitudes and an unfailing recognition of and gratitude for the many blessings that *must* come our way when we are obedient to the Lord's commands.

Time and again we see, not accounts of untold monetary riches being dumped at the feet of the faithful tithe payer, but of small and priceless miracles that instead deposit huge sums in the individual Saint's eternal account.

ATTITUDE, GRATITUDE AND HEAVENLY BLESSINGS

Time and again we see tales of an individual's battle with faith and obedience and trust. Sometimes these battles have been brief, other times decades long. Yet, invariably, for those who finally choose to take that step of faith, the ending is the same; He who is bound when we keep His commandments has opened the windows of heaven with those blessings for which the faithful Saint stands most in need.

There is a cycle that we traverse whenever we set out to be obedient to a commandment. In the instance of this book, it has been the commandment of paying tithes. First, the person has a desire to be obedient. That desire is followed by faith that, by doing that which the Lord has required, the Lord will then step in and come through and keep His part of the bargain. Faith is followed by works; paying the tithing. By paying a full and honest tithe, obedience has occurred. But the cycle does not end there, for the truly converted will then consciously look for and acknowledge the blessing(s) received and will convey gratitude to the Lord. An attitude of gratitude is the crowning step in obedience. As the Lord has taught,

> In nothing doth man offend God, or against none is his wrath kindled, save those who confess not his hand in all things, and obey not his commandments. (Doctrine & Covenants 59:21)

Nephi's accounts in the Book of Mormon give us a remarkable example, time and again, of a person seeing and most graciously acknowledging the Lord's hand in even the most demanding of circumstances.

On the ocean trek from Bountiful to the America's, Laman and Lemuel bind him with cords and treat him "with much harshness" for four long days. At last, he records

> ... wherefore, they came unto me, and loosed the bands which were upon my wrists, and behold they had swollen exceedingly; and also mine ankles were much swollen, and great was the soreness thereof.
>
> Nevertheless, I did look unto my God, and I did praise him all the day long; and I did not murmur against the Lord because of mine afflictions. (1 Nephi 18:15-16)

Even as Nephi, having proven the Lord "herewith," the wise person will build on that single step of faith with another step, and another, repeating the cycle of faith-obedience-acknowledgment-gratitude, until he has constructed a pattern of obedience and an attitude of gratitude that will stand him well through the eternities.

It is our hope that the accounts of faithful Saints in these latter-days will strengthen the reader's testimony of the blessings awaiting in regards to the law of tithes and offerings. Truly, the heavens stand so very ready and willing to

> ... prove me now herewith, saith the Lord of Hosts, if I will not open you the windows of heaven, and pour you out a blessing that there shall not be room enough to receive it. (3 Nephi 24:10-11)

ANITA HOLMES

Anita Holmes is Director of Community Development for Springdale, Utah (gateway community to Zion National Park), a free lance writer, and the only female certified fire marshal in the state of Utah.

Sister Holmes earned a bachelor's degree from Maryhurst and a Master of Public Administration degree from Lewis and Clark. Along with community service and Church activities, numerous writing projects and never-ending farm chores at her New Harmony, Utah home, she enjoys growing with and learning from her six children.

Johnda Mason Smith

Johnda Mason Smith and her husband Nicholas have four children and two grandchildren. Johnda has served as Primary President, Young Women's President, a counselor in the Relief Society, Ward Librarian, Ward Music Chairperson and on the Stake Primary Board.

She has also been heavily involved in community service. She served on the committee that organized the Block Home Program to protect the children in her community. She has volunteered in the school system as a tutor, an office aid, and is the Health Screening Facilitator for the High School. After being away from higher education for many years, she returned to school and majored in Psychology at Whitman College.